Secretary of the Treasury

Civil Service : Ireland: second report: Dublin Metropolitan Police

Secretary of the Treasury

Civil Service : Ireland: second report: Dublin Metropolitan Police

ISBN/EAN: 9783741105265

Manufactured in Europe, USA, Canada, Australia, Japa

Cover: Foto ©ninafisch / pixelio.de

Manufactured and distributed by brebook publishing software
(www.brebook.com)

Secretary of the Treasury

Civil Service : Ireland: second report: Dublin Metropolitan Police

REPORT

OF THE

COMMISSIONERS APPOINTED BY THE LORDS COMMISSIONERS OF HER MAJESTY'S TREASURY

TO ENQUIRE INTO THE CONDITION

OF

THE CIVIL SERVICE IN IRELAND

ON THE

DUBLIN METROPOLITAN POLICE;

TOGETHER WITH THE

MINUTES OF EVIDENCE

AND

APPENDICES.

Presented to both Houses of Parliament by Command of Her Majesty.

DUBLIN:
PRINTED BY ALEXANDER THOM, 87 & 88, ABBEY-STREET,
FOR HER MAJESTY'S STATIONERY OFFICE.

1873.

[C.—788.] *Price 8d.*

TABLE OF CONTENTS.

CIVIL SERVICE (IN IRELAND) ENQUIRY COMMISSION.

DUBLIN METROPOLITAN POLICE."

REPORT.

In conformity with the instructions conveyed to us by your Lordships' minute of the 16th September last, and upon the approval signified to us by Mr. Law's letter of the 11th October following, we have instituted a careful enquiry into the state of the Dublin Metropolitan Police Force.

Strength of force.

This Force was originally organized in 1837, and in 1838, when its duties actually commenced, it consisted of 911 officers and men. Since that time small additions to its numbers have been made, the particulars of which will be found in Appendix VI.

Vacancies.

The present authorized strength of the establishment is 1,096 men, including the rank of Superintendent, and there are 114 vacancies.

The condition of the Force was investigated by a Commission appointed by your Lordships' Board in the year 1866, and its history and organization will be found fully stated in their Confidential Report. The present rates of pay, with the exception of some trifling subsequent alterations, were then fixed.

Method of taking evidence.

We have examined several men of all grades in the Force (the men having been permitted by the Chief Commissioner to choose their own representatives to come before us), and we may state that no complaint of importance has been made to us of any grievance connected with either the organisation or administration of the body.

Notice of retirement.

The men of the Force have a right to resign upon giving a week's notice of their intention to do so.

Q. 103.

Voluntary resignations.

The Chief Commissioner has informed us that for the twelve months up to the 1st of October last, 82 *voluntary* resignations have occurred (of which number 72 are included in the current year); that the number of recruits available in the same period has been 80; and that a large number of the men who leave the Force go to the London Metropolitan and other police forces in England, where the pay is higher than in the Dublin Police.

Recruits.

Table A. in Appendix I. Appendix VI. and Q. 85.

Q. 75-77.

Rates of pay in England and Ireland.

The rates of pay at present in force are shown in the appendix, as also those which obtained in the London Metropolitan Police, and in the police forces of some of the principal cities and towns of England and Scotland, before the recent increase in the pay of the metropolitan body. A statement of the present pay of the London Metropolitan Police is given as well. A comparison will show that the pay of the Dublin Force is much less than that of the corresponding forces in the sister countries.

Tables C, D, E, F, in Appendix I. Appendix VII. and Appendix VIII.

Competition of England and Scotland with Ireland.

The facility of correspondence and communication brings the police of England and Scotland into direct competition for recruits with the Dublin Police, and the effect of this state of things is to offer strong inducements to young men of good character, as soon as they have learnt their duties, and become useful policemen, to leave Dublin and enlist in the police forces of other parts of the United Kingdom.

Qs. 75, 276, 278, 305-307 and Appendix

These inducements are not counteracted, to any appreciable extent, by a difference in the cost of living in favour of Dublin, as will appear from the following considerations relative to the expense of messing and rent :—

*This head includes the office of the Chief Commissioner, the Dublin Metropolitan Police Magistrates, and their offices.—See class III., Vote 30, of the Civil Service Estimates for 1872-3.

Messing in Dublin.

I. The Chief Commissioner compels the unmarried men, who all live in barracks, to mess together for one meal each day—the dinner—one of the men being appointed caterer.

Barrack expenses.

No complaint was made as to the expenditure on this meal, which amounts to 6s. 4d. each man per week. There is also a payment of 2s. 10d. per week for barrack expenses, giving a total weekly cost of living for each man of 9s. 2d.

Messing in Great Britain.

In Appendix VII., to which reference has been already made, will be found a tabulated return of the amount paid in London and other towns of England and Scotland for a similar provision, and it will be found that in London and most other places the cost is slightly less than in Dublin.

Rent in Dublin.

II. We have had, from the Chief Commissioner a return of the weekly rents paid by all the married men of the Dublin Metropolitan Police, and we find that the average amount paid by the constables and sub-constables is about 3s. a week.

Rents in London.

We have ascertained that in London about one-third of the Force have quarters provided for them in stations, or section houses; the maximum rates of rent payable in the case of married officers being—Inspectors, 5s. 6d.; Sergeants, 4s.; Constables, 3s. per week; extra rooms required by men with large families being paid for at the rate of 6d. per fifty superficial feet; and the evidence we have been able to obtain leads us to believe that the average cost of lodging in London, outside of these buildings, is about 5s. a week. While, therefore, the cost of rent is somewhat lower in Dublin than in London, that of messing is slightly higher, and the net difference in favour of the former is not sufficient, as above stated, to counteract the more evident advantages of the higher pay given in England.

We proceed to state *seriatim* the changes which we recommend should be made in the condition of the force, arranged under separate heads.

PAY.

Looking to the considerations already adverted to, we have arrived at the conclusion that there are no grounds for making the remuneration of a policeman less in Dublin than it is in London, but having regard to the difference, in favour of the former place, in the cost of lodging and the deduction hereafter referred to of 2½ per cent. which is made from the pay of the London Police, we think that a money payment slightly less in amount to the Dublin would be equivalent to that now given to the London constable.

At the same time we wish to remark that the rise in the price of the necessaries of life, the diminution in Ireland of the ranks of the population from which the police is recruited, and the increased demand for labour, have been so remarkable of late years, that we cannot undertake to recommend any scale of pay which will command a sufficient supply of properly qualified recruits for a given period in the future.

We beg leave to append, in parallel columns, the present rates of pay, and those which we recommend in their place :—

Margin references (right): Q. 31–36 2&c. 252. / Qs. 37, 238 244. / Qs. 26, 27. / Qs. 20–22 4&c. 164. / Q. 456, and Appendix VII. / Qs. 311, 312, 660, 846–848, 961–973, 1089, 1000, and Appendices I., II., and IX.

Weekly Pay.

	Present £ s. d.	Recommended £ s. d.	DETECTIVE DEPARTMENT. Present £ s. d.	Recommended £ s. d.
Supernumerary,	0 10 0	0 16 0		
Third Class Constable,	0 15 6	1 3 0		
Second Class Constable, Second Grade,	0 16 9	1 6 0		
Second Class Constable, First Grade,	0 17 6	1 7 6	0 18 0	1 8 6
First Class Constable,	0 19 0	1 9 0	1 0 0	1 10 0
Acting Sergeant,	1 0 0	1 12 6	1 2 0	1 13 6
Full „	1 5 0	1 14 6	1 5 0	1 14 6
Acting Inspector,	1 6 0	1 16 0	{ 1 7 6 { 1 8 6	1 18 0 1 19 0

Annual Pay.

	Present £ s. d.	Recommended £ s. d.		
Third Class Inspector,	107 0 0	137 0 0		
Second „ „	115 0 0	150 0 0	Inspector, £153	£180
First „ „	123 0 0	160 0 0		
Superintendents,	{ 180 0 0 to { 210 0 0	{ 220 0 0 to { 250 0 0	Superintendent, £210	£250
Chief Superintendent,	266 10 0	330 0 0		

We further recommend that the increased rates, as above proposed, should take effect from October 1st, 1872, and we make this suggestion with the greater confidence from a consideration of the circumstances under which this enquiry was entrusted to us, and of the patience and good conduct of the men pending the investigation.

Deduction for superannuation in London force.

In any comparison which may be made between the rates of pay in the Metropolitan Police of London and Dublin respectively, it must be remembered that a deduction of 2½ per cent. is made from the salaries of the former force, to provide a superannuation fund, while no such deduction is made from those of the latter.

See Appendix VIII.

ALLOWANCES.

Boots.

Under this head complaints have been made by the subordinate members of the force that no allowance is given for boots, which we find are supplied to the men of all the city police forces of England and Scotland.

Qs. 56, 61, 62, 208, 378, 450, and Appendix II.

We think this demand reasonable, and we recommend that an allowance of £1 12s. per annum for boots be given to all ranks below that of third class inspector.

Re-fitting clothing.

There is also a complaint that after a short period of wear, the uniforms of the force require to be refitted, which has now to be done at the expense of the men.

Qs. 54–58, and Appendix II.

We recommend that an allowance should be made to meet this expenditure, on a scale to be submitted by the Chief Commissioner, founded on an average of the actual cost.

Equipment of mounted men.

The mounted men of the force also ask for an allowance for spurs, spur boxes, and leather gloves, which we think should be conceded to them.

Q. 64. Appendix II.

Uniforms.

None of the subordinate officers above the rank of full sergeant are supplied with uniform. We recommend that uniforms, or allowances in place of them, should be given to all the officers under the rank of Assistant Commissioner, as is the usage generally in England.

Qs. 58, 214–216, 450.

Plain clothes of Detectives.

In the detective branch, we think that an allowance of 2s. per week should be given, to meet the cost of plain clothes, in conformity with the practice of the police forces in the large towns of England and Scotland.

Qs. 66, 67, 243–252.

Forage.

We have gone minutely into the present cost of horse-keeping, and we have come to the conclusion, that the allowance for the actual keep of a horse should be £45 a year. This is independent of the wages of a groom, and where it is provided by the present regulations, as in the case of the Superintendents of the Dublin Metropolitan Police, that a servant should be supplied, an additional sum of £45 ought to be allowed.

Qs. 171–172, (and see evidence to Royal Irish Constabulary). Q. 222.

Servants.

Assistant Commissioner.

The Assistant Commissioner has called our attention to the alleged insufficiency of his salary with regard to the position he fills, to the inadequacy of his forage allowance, and to the fact that he has no allowance for a servant.

See A. in Appendix IV., and Q. 170

We recommend that the forage allowance should be increased, as above proposed, to £45 a year, and we are further of opinion that his claim for an allowance for a servant is fair, and should be conceded.

Surgeon.

We think, looking to the extent of the district which he is obliged to visit, that the Surgeon of the Force should also have an allowance for travelling equivalent to that made for the keep of a horse.

Qs. 508, 519, 567.

Superintendents.

The Superintendents have now £25 a year to provide an office and stable. We think this insufficient, and recommend that the allowance should be increased to £30 a year when accommodation is not given.

Qs. 9, 317.

HOUSE ACCOMMODATION.

Practice as to lodging in Dublin.

The men are all obliged to lodge within their respective districts, their lodgings being periodically inspected. The Chief Commissioner complained very much of the effect produced on the health and efficiency of the men by the inferior character of the dwellings they are compelled to occupy.

Qs. 47, 48, 459 460, 538, 540.

Do. in England.

It appears that in many of the city police forces in England a practice has been adopted of providing blocks of buildings contiguous to the police station, for the purpose of affording lodgings at a reasonable rate to married men. This system is obviously attended with many advantages, both in reference to discipline and sanitary considerations, and it appears to us that it might be carried into effect without entailing any pecuniary charge on the public.

Qs. 467, 468.

Inspectors. The inspectors receive a lump sum for lodging, which is divided amongst Q. 9. them. We are of opinion that a fixed allowance of £20 a year should be made to each inspector who is not provided with quarters in the barracks.

RECRUITING.

Standard of height. The standard of height for recruits is 5 feet 9 inches. This seems to us Appendix I. unnecessarily high, and we cannot persuade ourselves that it does not diminish and Q 91. their supply, although it has been stated to us that it has been slightly reduced without increasing the number of men presenting themselves for entry into the force.

NOTICE OF RESIGNATION.

We recommend that the notice required on retirement from the Force should be extended from a week to a month.

OFFICE OF THE CHIEF COMMISSIONER.

Recommendations as to salary postponed. We have also instituted a careful inquiry, both by oral evidence and personal inspection, into the Office Establishment of the Chief Commissioner, and whilst we postpone recommending any change with regard to the salaries of the staff until we have investigated other clerical branches of the Civil Departments, we suggest that the following alterations may be made in the organisation of the Office:—

Accountant (so-called). I. The title of "Accountant," which at present designates the head of the Q. 175, 307, department, is calculated to convey an erroneous impression of the position of 335-340, 383, that officer. 504-508

Although he is responsible, under the Chief Commissioner, for the correctness of the accounts, his principal duties are those of correspondence and control, and we think that his designation should be that of "Chief Clerk."

Distribution of staff II. The disposition of the different clerks is at present as follows:—

(a.) The Accountant (or as above proposed, "Chief Clerk"), has two second- Q. 347. class clerks under him, for the correspondence and general duties of the office.

(b.) The "Finance Clerk," who is entrusted with the book-keeping and Qu. 347, 650- accounts, is assisted by another of the second-class clerks. 658.

(c.) The "Registrar of Cars," to whose branch the remaining two clerks are Q. 343. attached.

We are of opinion that the duties of one of the second-class clerks in the Qu. 195-197. Chief Clerk's department may be efficiently performed by a person in a position 397. analogous to that of a writer, and that, when a vacancy occurs, it would be advisable that it should be filled up by the introduction of a man taken from the Police Force.

The same recommendation extends to the posts of "Registrar of Cars," and Qu. 391-409, of his two subordinate clerks. The Registrar is entrusted with the receipt of 550-557. all the police revenue (arising from various sources), for the proper custody Qu. 389-365. of which he is obliged to give security. 385-606

Beyond this responsible duty, however, his functions, and those of his Qu. 588, 715 assistants, are of an ordinary and entirely mechanical character. 750.

Duties of Registrar of Cars may be undertaken by men selected from the Force. By the substitution of a system, which the Chief Commissioner has pre- See Appendix pared at our suggestion, and by which the carriage licences would be paid by VI. stamps, and the remainder of the revenue paid direct into the Bank of Ireland, all pecuniary responsibility on the part of the Registrar of Cars would be avoided, and the whole of the duties of his branch could be satisfactorily performed by persons taken from the Police Force.

Consequent reduction in expense. The employment of such men would effect a reduction in the salaries of the establishment, and would, at the same time, afford promotion to deserving and properly qualified members of the force.

DUBLIN METROPOLITAN POLICE MAGISTRATES.

Recommendations as to salary postponed. The case of the Police Magistrates and their clerks for an improvement Qu. 754-770. of salary is founded mainly on the alleged increase in the cost of living, and 820, 842-850 as this consideration applies to them in common with the members of the

Civil Service generally, we similarly postpone entertaining this branch of the subject until we shall have investigated the question on a broader basis.

No change in staff

We do not recommend any change in the present numbers and organisation of the staff.

PROPORTION OF COST BORNE BY LOCALITY.

We are fully alive to the fact that the recommendations we have made will increase the cost of the force.

Present contributions from Imperial and local funds.

This expenditure is now met by the Imperial Exchequer, supplemented by various local sources of revenue, and by a rate on the Dublin Metropolitan District, the maximum of which is fixed at 8*d.* in the pound. The amount derived from this rate might, we have reason to believe, be largely increased by a re-valuation of the property liable to it.

Might be re-adjusted.

It may be worth the consideration of the Government, whether it would not *Qs. 541-549.* be right, looking to the increased cost of the force, the advancing prosperity of the district for which it is provided, and the precedent of the analogous English and Scotch bodies of Police, to review and re-arrange the proportions in which the Imperial Exchequer and the local rates contribute to the expense of this service.

MONCK.

MYLES O'REILLY.

S. A. BLACKWOOD.

November 29, 1872.

DUBLIN METROPOLITAN POLICE.

LIST OF WITNESSES.

LIST OF PAPERS IN APPENDIX.

CIVIL SERVICE (IN IRELAND) ENQUIRY COMMISSION, 1872.

TREASURY MINUTE, Dated 16th September, 1872.

The Chancellor of the Exchequer states to the Board, that in fulfilment of the pledge given by him in the House of Commons, during the debate which took place on the 30th of April last, upon the subject of the condition of the Civil Service in Ireland, he submits that an inquiry into the state of that service should, as suggested by the Irish Government, be intrusted to the Right Hon. Lord Monck, Myles William O'Reilly, esq., M.P. and S. A. Blackwood, esq., an officer of the Treasury, and that they should proceed to Dublin for that purpose.

The Chancellor of the Exchequer proposes that the Commission above named should, after conference with the Chief Secretary for Ireland, report to the Treasury for approval the names of the departments into which they propose first to inquire.

As regards the course of the inquiry, the Chancellor of the Exchequer proposes that they should inquire into and report on the rates of pay received by the civil servants in each of the departments which they examine, and should state whether, in their opinion, such rates are sufficient to secure the services of properly qualified persons.

In judging rates of pay, they should be guided by the following considerations:—

1. That the officers of the Civil Service in Ireland should be paid a fair price for the work required of them, but not a higher price than that for which the Government can get the work efficiently performed.

2. They should obtain information of the ordinary scale of remuneration which obtains in Dublin for professional and commercial work, requiring in their judgment similar qualifications as to education, attainments, and responsibility.

3. In comparisons founded on the last inquiry, they should bear in mind the uninterrupted and progressive character of the Government pay, the hours of attendance, the practice as to sick leave, and the pension on retirement.

4. They should institute some independent inquiry as to the rate at which the local cost of living has increased since the time when the present rates of salaries were fixed.

5. It will not be the duty of the Commissioners to investigate any merely personal grievances, which may be brought before them, but they will report what, in their opinion, are the causes of such dissatisfaction as may be said to exist in any of the services referred to them

6. They should ascertain whether any of the departments are overmanned, and if so, recommend such reductions in numbers as may appear advisable.

Mr. Horace Seymour, an officer of the Treasury, will attend the Commission and act as secretary.

My Lords approve. Let the necessary directions be given accordingly.

October 21, 1872.

The Commissioners appointed by the above Treasury Minute met to-day for the first time, and deliberated as to the course of their enquiry.

MINUTES OF EVIDENCE.

DUBLIN METROPOLITAN POLICE.

October 22, 1872.

The Commissioners sat at half-past ten o'clock this morning, and proceeded with the examination of witnesses.

Colonel Henry Atwell Lake, C.B., examined.

1. Lord Monck.—What is your name and your office?—Colonel Lake, Chief Commissioner of the Dublin Metropolitan Police.

2. There is a certain amount of discontent existing in the force which has diminished its numbers very considerably?—There is.

3. And you have made a report to the Government, containing your views upon the subject?—Yes.

4. And you put that report in as part of your evidence?—Yes. (See Appendix No. I.)

5. You also put in this memorial from the men of the Metropolitan Police to you as their Chief?—Yes. (See Appendix No. II.)

6. Will you tell us the different grades in the force from yourself down to the rank of constable—then we will ask you what you suppose to be the pressing grievance of each respective grade?—Yes.

7. What we want, is first a statement of the different grades; have you got that?—Yes.

8. Will you state the different grades in the force, beginning with yourself and going downwards?—The Chief Commissioner at £1,000 a year; £40 for a horse and man, and £150 house-rent; the Assistant Commissioner, £600 a year; £40 for a horse and man, but no house-rent. I suppose I had better give you the actual pay received without the stoppages.

9. We want to see now the actual position of the force, we can get the other afterwards?—The Chief Superintendent, including all allowances, £454 10s.; the Superintendents, including horse allowance and

B 2

October 22.
Colonel Henry
Atwell Lake,
&c.

everything else, on an average about £288 each;* Inspectors, first class, £123 a year; second class, £115; and third class, £107 a year. All those inspectors who are not provided with quarters are granted lodging money in this way. There is one amount of £145 annually divided amongst them, but they don't all get it. It gives about £8 a year to each of those who are not provided with a lodging. The next rank, that of acting inspector, receives weekly (the others were annually), £1 6s. ; the sergeants, £1 3s. ; the acting sergeants, £1 each ; constables, first rate 19s. ; second rate, 17s. 6d. ; third rate, 16s 9d. ; fourth rate, 15s. 6d., and supernumeraries, 10s. each, weekly. Would you like to have the pay of the Superintendents and their allowances separately?

10. If you please?—There is £464 10s for the Chief Superintendent, made up in this way :—His ordinary pay is £286 10s, and then he gets allowances for forage, and groom, and house rent. The pay of the Superintendents is £210 annually, and £78 for forage, groom, and horse.

11. Mr. BLACKWOOD—The Chief Superintendent gets a personal allowance of £50 ?—Yes, he got that for his services during the Fenian excitement, but the man who comes after him will have £100 a year less, because he got £50 a year granted to him for special services, on two separate occasions—so that he gets £100 a year personal allowance as a reward for special services, which his successor will not receive. Then as to the detective force ; the Chief Superintendent is the chief of that branch, and I have given his pay. There is one inspector with £152 19s. 8d. a year ; the acting inspectors, £1 8s. 6d. a week, and £1 1s. 6d. a week, sergeants, £1 5s. a week ; acting sergeants, £1 3s ; constables, £1 and 18s.

12. I see by the estimates that there are six different rates of pay for constables ?—In the Dublin police?

13. Yes; these are the estimates for this year?—There are only four rates that I know of. (On reference to the estimates it was seen that the six rates comprised the detective and ordinary constables.)

14. Lord MONCK.—Can you give a statement of the comparative rates of pay of the London and the Dublin Metropolitan Police?—Yes—of the London Metropolitan and City Police.

15. Is the pay of the London Metropolitan and the City Police different?—Yes, and their pay is a great deal higher than that of the Dublin Police.

16. Yes, I know it is. The statement which you have handed in shows the relations, in point of pay and emoluments, between the Dublin Metropolitan Police and the London Police?—Yes. [This is shown in the return marked "C" with Appendix No. I.]

17. Don't you think with such a statement as that, it is unnecessary to take into consideration all the minute particulars gone into in this memorial?—Yes, and I should not have retained all that is in that memorial but that I think the men would not have been satisfied otherwise.

18. The memorial states that the duty is very much heavier with the Dublin than with the London police; the number of offenders they arrested is given, which is very considerable—about half as many as by the police in London, who in number are nine times as large?—Yes.

19. And the pay of the London police is much larger evidently than that of the police here?—Yes.

20. Of course there may be a difference in the cost of living; if so, that would modify the comparison?—I have got a statement here showing that the cost of living here is quite as dear as in London. For instance, we mess the men for 5s. 6d. a week, and the mess in London is about the same. I mess my men in barracks—I am speaking of the unmarried men—at 5s. 6d. a week—that is dinner only. That does not include Friday, on which day, you are aware, they don't eat meat, and on that day they pay 10d. for eggs and fish, making up altogether about 6s. 4d. That does not include breakfast, tea, or supper ; but in London, I am informed, that they mess the men there for 5s. 6d. the whole seven days.

21. Mr. BLACKWOOD.—Only their dinners in London?—Yes; only their dinners.

22. Lord MONCK.—Do you believe that is true. Can you assure us of that; because it is a very important point?—Yes ; but Dr. Nedley, who is the physician to the force, has gone over to London, and got all the information. I believe he has got also information with reference to the police in Liverpool, Manchester, Birmingham, and Glasgow, and I think it would be better to have the information from himself. Then as regards lodgings—there is an immense deal of difference in that. My married men all live in lodgings, which they have to provide and pay for themselves.

23. And for which there is no allowance made them?—No, no allowance at all.

24. What provision is there in the police force here with regard to lodgings for the unmarried and the married men?—All single men live in barracks, and for that there is a certain stoppage made every week, for their lodging, washing, cooking, &c.

25. What is the stoppage for lodging?—1s. 2d for lodging and fuel.

26. Mr. O'REILLY.—A week?—Yes. The 1s. 2d. is for lodging and fuel—8d. for lodging, and 6d. for fuel ; washing shirts, sheets, and stockings, 10d.

27. That is expenditure and not stoppage?—No, it is actually stopped. They pay cooks' wages, 3d. a week ; and soap, &c., 3d. a week.

28. Is that a regulation stoppage?—The actual stoppages made from the pay, and which appear on the pay-sheets, are the following, viz. :—Lodging and fuel, sheet-washing, and also, as occasion requires, fines and deductions for sickness ; the other expenses which I have enumerated, are paid by the constables on pay-day, but none of them can be regarded as optional.

PAY and ALLOWANCES of the SUPERINTENDENTS.

Divisions.	Present Annual Pay.			Allowances.			Total.			
	£	s.	d.	£	s.	d.	£	s.	d.	
A,	180	0	0	78	0	0	258	0	0	Advancing by £5 a year to £210, maximum salary, exclusive of allowances.
B,	210	0	0	78	0	0	288	0	0	
C,	180	0	0	103	0	0	283	0	0	Same as above, and allowances include £25 a year for rent of office.
D,	210	0	0	131	5	0	341	5	0	Allowances include £25 a year for rent of office, and £18 5s. a year for car-hire.
E,	193	0	0	131	5	0	319	5	0	Same; salary not yet arrived at maximum.
F.	198	0	0	78	0	0	276	0	0	Salary not yet arrived at maximum.

NOTE.—The Superintendents of C, D, and E divisions are each allowed £25 a year for rent of an office, not being provided with one; and the Superintendents of D and E divisions are allowed 1s. each, per day, for car-hire, one horse being insufficient, owing to the extent of their divisions.

Metropolitan Police Office, Castle, 22nd November, 1872.

HENRY ATWELL LAKE, the Commissioner of Police.

29. Lord MONCK.—That is the state of the case as regards the unmarried men?—Yes.

30. Now, will you state the case with regard to the married men as to lodgings?—They have to pay for their lodgings, and I have a statement here as to how much they pay throughout the whole force.

31. Mr BLACKWOOD.—Is the cost of messing which you stated to be 5s. 6d. per week, and with Friday 6s. 4d., a stoppage from their pay?—Yes, they are obliged to pay it.

32. They pay 6s. 4d. a week stoppage for their dinner?—Yes, for their dinner only; I only oblige them to mess as regards their dinner. Breakfast, tea, and supper they can have as they like at their own option.

33. Is the stoppage for the messing compulsory?—Yes, it is; soon after I arrived here I found the practice existed of men messing themselves, and the consequence was that many of them did not eat a sufficient amount of meat to enable them to go through the hard work that they had to encounter. I therefore instituted the system of messing, and made it compulsory on the men as regards dinner only. One man is appointed messman every six months in each of the barracks. He goes to the market, buys the meat and vegetables, and has them dressed by the cook attached to the barrack, and the men sit down at a certain hour and eat as much as they can possibly want. In fact, it is the only meal they have in the day regularly and together.

34. Lord MONCK.—Do I understand you to mean, that this messing applies to the married and the unmarried men?—No; only the unmarried men; the married men live in their lodgings, as they like.

35. This messing system does not apply to the married men?—No; it does not apply to them.

36. Why not?—From the insufficiency of their pay. Many of them have large families—too large to enable them to afford meat every day.

37. Do the unmarried men complain of the cost of their messing?—When I first established the system it was not very popular among all of them, it was so with some, but not with all. But by degrees, when they saw the benefit that was derived from it, they got to like it very much, and became perfectly reconciled to it.

38. Has the cost increased of late, and have you been obliged to raise the rate of what is stopped; is it now more than or as much as when you first established the system?—I can hardly answer that now.

39. How long has this system been in operation?—I could not say now, but it is more than eight years. I should not like to answer that until I make inquiry.

40. Mr. BLACKWOOD.—Can you say whether the cost of messing has increased since the system was established?—I should like to answer that question after inquiry; but I think it must have been slightly, on account of the increase in the price of meat, but not so much in proportion to the increase in the price of meat, because they purchase it by contract, and the butchers supply the men with large quantities at much more reasonable rates than the general public.*

41. But do you fix the rate for the whole year, or do you, upon an examination of the accounts, divide the total cost?—No; it is liable to be altered if there is any necessity for it.

42. Upon your authority?—Yes.

43. And it does not need the sanction of the Irish Government?—Oh, dear, no.

44. The arrangement is made entirely between yourself and the force?—It is entirely a matter between myself and the force.

45. But there are no objections raised to it now?—No; not the least objection. I never heard a word from any of the men, and I very often go round the messes to see them.

46. Lord MONCK.—That is the case of the unmarried men?—Yes.

47. They are provided with barracks, and they mess together in that way, but the married men are not compelled to mess, and they find their own lodgings, without any allowance?—Yes; and their lodgings are periodically inspected by the clothing sergeant, or barrack sergeant, and if they are not living in proper places, they are reported to me.

48. You, in fact, exercise a control over them, as regards the houses they live in?—Yes; and each man is obliged to live in his own division—they are not allowed to live where they like—they must live within a certain circle. I have here a statement as regards every man who is married in the force, of how much rent he pays for his lodgings, the number of rooms he occupies, and whether they are healthy or not.

49. That statement applies to the present time?—Yes; it was only recently made.

50. Have you any similar statement for past years?—No; but I have the prices of lodgings in Birmingham, Manchester, and Glasgow here, to show the difference.†

51. Mr. BLACKWOOD.—Do you know whether the same system of messing prevails in the London Metropolitan Police?—Yes; I think it does.

52. Lord MONCK.—Well, so far with regard to habitations and food. But I see in the memorial that there is a certain amount of complaint about clothing, and allowances in reference to it?—Yes.

53. Is any allowance made in the way of clothing, independent of pay?—Up to the rank of inspector uniforms are provided. The inspectors and superintendents clothe themselves. Last year or the year before I applied to the Treasury, through Government, for leave to give the inspectors helmets, which was allowed. Before that they always wore their own hats, and they looked very bad. Helmets are given to the superintendents and inspectors, but no clothing. But in London the inspectors and superintendents get a clothing allowance.

54. Mr. BLACKWOOD.—It is only certain articles of clothing that your men get?—Yes; they have to find their own boots. That is a heavy item of expense, they pay 16s. a pair for them. The men will wear out two pairs by constant walking in the year, and there is also something for repairs. There is another charge I would wish to refer to, and that is one to which they are subject for altering their clothes, and from which they would be very gladly relieved. When the contractor brings the clothing he has it fitted on every man, and I myself or the Assistant Commissioner inspect them; but a man's clothing often after a heavy rain, or after having been worn for some time, gets out of shape, and then he has to have it altered to make it fit for wear at his own expense. That does not cost very much—only a few shillings—but they complain of it very bitterly.

55. What articles of clothing are supplied to the men?—Helmets, tunics, trousers, great-coats, capes, and gaiters. They get no under-clothing at all.

56. Mr. O'REILLY.—What would you propose with reference to the cost of changing the clothing: in the first instance the clothes are fitted to the men?—They are.

57. What do you propose as to the cost of subsequent alterations?—You know that it does not do for a policeman, who requires the free use of his arms, to be tightened up like a soldier, and therefore the clothes are made rather larger than is absolutely necessary; but then the clothes shrink from rain and exposure, and they don't fit as they ought to do. Little alterations have to be made, for which they have to pay themselves. I think these alterations ought to be paid for out of the contingent account kept by the superintendent, who could charge for them. If it were charged in the contingent account that would be a very great relief to the men, and would not be a very heavy item.

58. Lord MONCK.—Might not the difficulty be met

* See reply to question 544. † See Appendix No. VII., where this information is given.

in this way; by taking an average, and allowing 1s. or 2s. a man?—Yes; I could very easily get an average.

59. Mr. O'REILLY.—Is there any contingent account properly so called, the amount of which is not accounted for, like the contingent allowance in the army?—The superintendent of each division has what they call a contingent account—for instance, if he sends a man away in a great hurry to a place where it is necessary for him to go he pays the hire of an outside car.

60. That is a contingent account for which you must account by items, but there is a contingent account in the army, which is not accounted for in that way?—There is no such contingent account with us.

61. The men have to supply themselves with boots and all under-clothing?—Yes.

62. Would it be an advantage to the men if they were supplied with them at regulation prices, like soldiers, from Government stores?—Yes; I would suggest that they ought to be so supplied. The men would prefer to have the allowance, but I would prefer to have them supplied. My men tell me they pay 16s. a pair for boots, which presses very hardly upon them.

63. Soldiers are supplied from the army stores with all these articles of clothing, with boots, shirts, and socks. These are all supplied upon large contracts at much less than men can purchase them for if purchased singly in shops?—There is no doubt of that at all.

64. Lord MONCK.—We have now got your opinion with respect to the habitation, food, and clothing of the men; is there anything else you would like to add?—Yes; the horse policemen, or mounted police complain that they have to supply themselves with spurs and spur boxes, and with leather gloves, which the other men do not wear. The other men wear cotton gloves, and the mounted men complain that they are obliged to wear leather gloves, and also wear out more shirts, and I dare say they do. They also complain that they have a better description of boots to provide. They also sent in a memorial stating that as the Cavalry and mounted police of the Royal Irish Constabulary had a small increase of pay beyond the ordinary men, the mounted men of our force consider they have a claim to a small increase of pay also.

65. The mounted men of your force get no increase?—No; none whatever.

66. From the memorial here we find that the detective portion of the force are obliged to provide themselves with a description of clothing that the ordinary police do not require?—Yes; and that is because they are always in plain clothes. They are also obliged to have a suit of uniform, because on occasions when they go up as witnesses in the courts they are in uniform; otherwise they wear plain clothes.

67. You think that their increased pay is insufficient to cover their increased expenditure in that respect?—They have always asked for an increase of pay on the plea that it does not; and I really think it a justifiable demand, for they are often obliged to be very well dressed, and to wear certain clothes which on ordinary occasions they would not do, in order to disguise themselves a little.

68. Mr. BLACKWOOD.—Is there any complaint on the ground of pensions?—Yes, there is. I think that is all embodied in this memorial.

69. Are the pensions fixed by Act of Parliament?—They are. The 30th and 31st Victoria, cap. 95, passed in 1867 as to all appointments to the force since it was passed. Will you allow me to tell you what the pensions were and are? In the 10th and 11th Victoria, cap. 100, passed in 1847, constables appointed after the Act was passed, above fifteen and under twenty years' service, may get half pay; above twenty and under twenty-five, two-thirds; above twenty-five and under thirty, three-fourths; and above thirty years' service, full pay. For appointments up to the date the Act was passed, fifteen and under twenty years' service, two-thirds of pay was prescribed; and above

twenty years, full pay. Then there was two per cent on account of superannuations deducted from the pay of all the men who were appointed after the Act of 1847 was passed. The Act of 1867 did away with the deduction, and these are the regulations it made as to appointments since it was passed:—After fifteen years' service, fifteen-fiftieths of the pay to be allowed as a retiring pension, and one-fiftieth for each successive year up to thirty years, when they get thirty-fiftieths.*

70. Is there no pension granted for any service under fifteen years?—No; not under fifteen years, except for injuries received in the service.

71. There are exceptions?—There are exceptions, and larger pensions may be granted in cases of extraordinary merit. That is in cases referred to the Treasury. "Pensions for full pay may be granted for injuries received in the execution of duty."

72. Lord MONCK.—Are you aware of the pensions of the London police?—I should say they are not regulated in the same way—they are not under the same Act.

73. Mr BLACKWOOD.—You have not given us any rate of pensions beyond fifteen years?—Yes; I stated one-fiftieth for each successive year over fifteen years. The men do not like the change in the pension at all. It had a great effect on them.

74. But if the pay of the Dublin police were assimilated to that of the London Metropolitan police, the pensions would have no effect in withdrawing men from the force?—No; I think if they were to be put on the same footing—which I beg most respectfully to suggest should be done—as regards pay of the London police, and provision made in respect of lodgings for married men, I am sure they would be satisfied.

75. You stated in the report you made to the Lord Lieutenant that you found considerable inconvenience from men leaving to go into the London and other police forces?—Yes, it is quite true. I dare say you are aware that I am 110 men below my strength, which, in so small a force, is a great deal, and although the force is put down at 1,066, the actual number of constables is very little more than 800. There is an area of 30 square miles to be looked after, and the percentage of constables when at the full strength to the population is one in 400 odd, or between 400 and 500. Often when I found the men going away from the service—men of six and eight years' standing—I found them going away very fast—I have sent for them, and had them up before me. I have sent for one whom he has sent in his resignation, and resigned at the end of a week. I have reasoned and talked with him. I have asked him the reason of his going, and if he had any complaints to make of the hardships of the service, as regards the discipline. I am always ready to grant an interview with regard to that, and I always encourage the men to come up to me direct. When I find the man of six or eight years' standing going away so very fast, I take the opportunity of sending for them to ask the reason, and on every single occasion there was not one man that did not complain of insufficiency of pay, that he was not able to have one good meal a day, and he had only to receive a good character from me on going away, and he would immediately be taken into the London or Liverpool police. From the applications I have received from the Commissioner in London, and the Chief of Police in Liverpool, and the Birmingham Chief Constable, I know that they are quickly taken up there.

76. Lord MONCK.—Did the men who left you enter some other police force?—Generally; but, of course, there were some occasions in which they did not. There were none of them who complained of the hardship of the service, or the strictness of their discipline, or anything of that sort. They had made up their minds to remain in the force, only the guinea a week took them elsewhere.

77. In fact, the conditions of the police force were not the cause of their leaving, but the desire to better themselves?—No; it was not the conditions of the police. On many occasions I argued with them, and said

* See also B. in Appendix No. I.

that there was a better day for them here, and after I was able to show, by the Lord Lieutenant's communication, that a Special Commission would sit, there was an improvement. I issued a notice to the force in August, and told them I was sure they would have their pay increased, and be put on a proper footing. Some who were going said, "Very well, if the pay is increased, and the force put on a proper footing, will you allow us to come back again?" I said that would be a matter for consideration. I said that I thought they should not go away with the prospect of better pay in a few months, and they said that they could not stay on the pay—that they could not live on it—that some of them had wives and children, and that they were really often a week without a bit of meat to eat. I believe that to be the case.

78. Is it necessary for a man to get leave to marry in your force?—Yes.

79. Is it a habit of your office to restrict marriage much?—No; as a general principle, I won't enlist a married man unless in the case of a man proving to me he has means of his own, or that his wife's relations have, nor do I allow a man to marry until he has been a certain time in the force to enable him to get into a high grade. Then I allow him to marry; but, first of all, I inquire into the character of the young woman, and then into their means, and as a rule I require a constable to produce £30, and his wife the same. That is to enable him to furnish his house. But if he marry without leave, I immediately dismiss him.

80. As I understand you, the restrictions as to marriage are confined exclusively to the condition of the man's means, as to whether he is able to support a wife, and not on any other ground?—Yes; and the respectability of the young woman.

81. Mr. BLACKWOOD.—I suppose that the resignations generally take place at an early period of a man's service?—You will hardly see a man that has been several years in the force resign, he looks forward to a pension; and when I first came to the force I hardly ever had a resignation of a man with over a couple of years' service. Lately I have had them with seven or eight years' service.

82. Mr. O'REILLY.—Could you say how many resignations you have had within the last couple of years?—Yes; shall I give them by the months?

83. Give us the total?—Seventy-two from January to September, 1879. I have not got up to October yet.

84. Lord MONCK.—That is at the rate of ten per cent. of the force for the whole year?—Yes.

85. Mr. BLACKWOOD.—And what was the longest service of those?—Of those who resigned?

86. Yes?—I don't think I have that here; but I have got the services of all the men in the force.

87. Mr. O'REILLY.—But you know that some of them had six or seven years' service?—Yes; I know that.

88. Lord MONCK.—Did you find it difficult to supply the places of those who resigned?—I did, for a long time; but after the notification of the Commission matters improved.

89. But before the notification announced there would be an inquiry. We want it before that as well as after?—I had very great difficulty; hardly a man came in, and those who did come and offer themselves as recruits were inferior in every respect.

90. Mr. O'REILLY.—Inferior in what respects?—In physique, in education, and other ways.

91. Lord MONCK.—You have rather a high standard of height?—Five feet nine inches; but I have latterly taken men who were only five feet eight and a half inches in the hope of their growing up another half inch by the drill.

92. Mr. BLACKWOOD.—In whose hands is the recruiting?—Wholly in mine.

93. I mean which of the subordinate officers is intrusted with it. Is there a recruiting staff?—None. It is not managed in that way. When Mr O'Ferrall, the late commissioner was here I did it wholly myself. But now the assistant commissioner has the recruit brought to him, and if there is any doubt about the

man—about his character, or anything of that sort—the assistant commissioner applies to me to know what I wish done.

October 22.
Colonel Henry Atwell Lake, c.b.

94. And how are the wants of the force made known with regard to recruits, is it by advertisement?—Within the last two or three months I have thought it well to advertise in the local papers all over Ireland, and it has had a very good effect; I have got many applications since.

95. But that is since the nomination of the Commission?—Yes.

96. But before the announcement of the Commission did you observe that there was any increase in the number of applications for admission?—I can hardly say whether it was before or at the time, but it may be assumed that, generally speaking, not much was known about the Commission in the provinces.

97. Mr. O'REILLY.—But a great part has been since the issuing of the advertisements?—Yes; and also since the notification of the commission.

98. Mr. BLACKWOOD.—Is there any change in the method of recruiting? Is there any bounty offered?—Oh, no; the only alteration I made was this:—On the previous ordinary occasions, when a man came up to present himself as a recruit, he paid his own expenses whether he was taken or rejected, but in the advertisement I issued, I offered to pay the expenses, third class fare by rail, to any who should be enlisted; if he was rejected by the doctor he paid his own expenses.

99. Is it possible for any of the force—the subordinate officers or men, to accelerate or retard enlistment?—I do not think they would retard it, but I had an idea that they might assist me, and that the men going on leave—whether their usual or sick leave—might help me by inducing their friends to come up. And I applied to the government to be allowed to give any man who brought up a recruit that passed the examination £1, but it was refused.

100. Mr. O'REILLY.—But I should take it, that one reason for the refusal by government was, that they knew that any man after passing could give a week's notice after getting the £1, and leave?—But he would not get the £1; it was paid the man who brought him up.

101. But it might be done by arrangement between friends?—I don't know as to that.

102. Lord MONCK.—Do you think it possible that the force, having those grievances to complain of, and wishing to put pressure on the Government, try to discourage enlistment?—I do not think that for one moment. There is one thing I would wish to state. The regulations are, that the men who wish to leave, need only give a week's notice. I think the notice ought to be made a month, as it is in the constabulary.

103. Mr. O'REILLY.—Do you still hold the rule of not accepting men from the city of Dublin?—I have been obliged to give that rule up lately, although I very much objected to do so. I object to a man belonging to the city, and having his friends always about him. However, now and then, when I would know a man who is of unexceptionably good character, I have taken him, although in former years I never did so. I object to take domestic servants. I object very much to old soldiers, for I find that they never will keep straight. They will drink; and I also object, although I sometimes take them, to men from the sister force, the Royal Irish Constabulary, for this reason, that the discipline in Dublin is so very different, they hardly ever remain, it does not agree with them. I like best to get the man with the frieze coat on him, and with the fingers that have been in the habit of using the spade.

104. Mr. BLACKWOOD.—I see by the regulations that when a man is ill there is a sick stoppage of a shilling a day?—Yes.

105. Is that enforced in all cases?—That stoppage is enforced unless the illness is the result of injuries received in the service, or that the doctor certifies that the money is absolutely required in order to keep him

October 22.
Colonel Henry
Atwell Lake,
C.B.

up, and to supply sufficient nourishment to him after illness.

106. Don't you think it hard for a man to be put under stoppages of pay when his illness is caused by exposure in the service?—I think it is very hard indeed, and when I came here first it was universally adopted. Mr. O'Ferrall, who had been a long while in the force, and I argued the point. I wished the stoppages of this kind removed, and said I considered it very hard indeed to stop a shilling a day from a man because he was ill. "Well," he said, "you may try it if you like, but you will find an immense deal of 'malingering' going on, and it is almost impossible for us or for the doctor to find out whether the man is sick or not." I know, from my experience in the army, how men will malinger if they can, and I adopted Mr. O'Ferrall's views, of course exercising my own judgment in certain cases. In later years I have relaxed that rule, and indeed I hardly ever stop it, unless in the case of a man who is constantly on the sick list.

107. Where are your men treated?—In the various hospitals, unless a man has only a headache or a cold, and then he is treated in his own house or the barracks.

108. Do you think that the same difficulty applies with regard to distinguishing illness in hospitals as would apply to illness when the man stops at his own residence—do you mean to say it would be more necessary to enforce the regulation on the man who remained at his lodgings, and therefore not positively invalided, or on the one you are sure has been positively invalided?—I think it depends very much upon the nature of the case. If a man is not ill enough to go to hospital, but is unable to go out on duty, and remains in the barracks it is generally only a matter of two or three days for him. But if he is ill enough to go to hospital it is generally a case of a month or six weeks for him.

109. But don't you know that the man in hospital is a more bond fide case than the man in lodgings?—But when he goes to hospital he is taken care of and fed.

110. As I understand you, you exercise a large discretion with regard to putting men on sick stoppages?—Yes. When a man who has had fever comes out of hospital and wishes to leave for the country to recruit his health, than if the doctor, on his certificate, recommends him for full pay I invariably adopt it. If the medical officer recommends the man for full pay it is given him when we are advised that he is in a weak state of body coming out of hospital, and requires to be fed up, and his constitution improved. On the doctor's certificate I order full pay. I always adopt it. I never go against it.

111. Is there any leave granted to the men?—The superintendents get a month if they wish for it; but they don't always ask for it. The men get ten days in the year, and are allowed full pay.

112. Is there very much difference between your force and the London Metropolitan Police as to the amount of leave granted the men?—I don't know.

113. How are the promotions in the force managed here?—Wholly by myself. I have a competitive examination when I have vacancies for acting sergeants. The men of the first rate coming up for examination. The first rate men come up to be examined, and are promoted accordingly, and wholly by myself.

114. And by means of examination?—By means of competitive examination, and other things combined with it.

115. Do men, therefore, all rise from the lowest grade up, and how high?—Constables are promoted from one rate to another by seniority, except a man has anything against him, such as drunkenness or the like; then he is passed over. From the rank of first-rate constable up to that of acting-sergeant he undergoes an examination, not only as to his literary qualification, but as to his efficiency as a police constable, which I hear from the officer under whom he served. I generally have a certain number of these who come up for examination on an approved list, and then they are promoted from that approved list. If a man behaves ill in the meanwhile, his name is erased.

116. Mr. O'REILLY.—Are they promoted by seniority from that list?—Yes, then from acting to full sergeant they go by seniority with the same exceptions.

117. Lord MONCK.—Character counts all through?—Yes; then from the rank of sergeant to acting-inspector they have another examination, and a certain number are put on an approved list, and taken from that list as vacancies occur. From acting-inspector to full inspector they go up by gradation, by seniority.

118. From sergeants to acting-inspectors and inspectors promotion is made by competitive examination?—We always have competitive examination. All the sergeants send in their names, the names are submitted to me, and if I see a man that I do not think is eligible, I erase his name.

119. Mr. BLACKWOOD.—Examination in writing or drill, or what?—In writing from dictation, arithmetic, geography of Ireland, and making out an imaginary report on any subject I give them. I make it all out myself and seal it up, and it is opened in the presence of the men by the instructor and another officer who are present to see the men do not copy from each other.

120. From inspector to the superintendent?—Promotion according to my idea of the qualifications of the men; there is no examination.

121. Mr. O'REILLY.—Am I right in concluding—to put it shortly—that from inspector to superintendent promotion is by selection?—By selection.

122. And that in the other stages it is either by seniority or by competitive examination amongst all men not disqualified?—Yes.

123. You do not select men independent of this examination?—No, in all this I give the man the benefit of the examination.

124. The two heads of your force, I believe, Colonel Lake, are yourself and Captain Talbot?—Yes.

125. And you both were strangers to the force? I mean you were not regular police officers. You were not promoted from the ranks?—Oh, no.

126. And I believe I may say that of every police force in the three kingdoms, so far as the head places are concerned?—Yes; that is to say, we do not rise from the ranks.

127. With that exception are all your officers promoted from the force itself?—Every one.

128. That has been the case since the commencement?—From the very commencement. I think there was one man brought in as chief superintendent who was not in the force originally, but that was long before my time.

129. May I ask your opinion on that. Do you consider that a good and satisfactory plan?—I should like the chief superintendent to be an independent man.

130. With that exception you are satisfied the police force can supply sufficient officers for itself?—I think so. I think it would be a dangerous thing to shut out these promotions.

131. Lord MONCK.—I think that the purport of your answer is, that the efficiency of the force does not require that the mode of promotion should be changed?—Yes.

132. Mr. BLACKWOOD.—Do you consider promotion sufficiently rapid in the force?—I do.

133. There is no undue stagnation?—No.

134. Mr. O'REILLY.—I see that the Treasury Commissioners, who reported in 1866, express their opinion that the number of officers in proportion to the number of men in the Dublin police force is larger than necessary, and they recommended a reduction at the time?—Yes.

135. Do you know has any change taken place in the proportion?—No; none.

136. You don't think you are over-officered?—No; I don't think so.

137. Am I not right in thinking that the proportion of officers to men in a military force does not apply to the police. A sergeant may be called a non-commissioned officer. Is a sergeant a working man in the police force?—He is; he keeps constantly going round the section visiting the men, but while on duty he

has, if the occasion arises, to act as a constable and make an arrest, and it is often done.

138. Lord Monck.—You have been talking of promotion, may I ask how are the punishments inflicted?—Do you mean to say the nature of the punishments, or how?

139. No; how is punishment inflicted—how is an adjudication in a case brought about?—Once a week, on Tuesday—I am giving it to you as it is at present; when I came here it was different—the Commissioner or Assistant Commissioner sits in what we call the Board-room, all the superintendents being present. Any defaulter, as we call him, who has been guilty of any crime—either drunkenness, or neglect of duty, or being dirty, or walking his beat in a slovenly manner, is put on the sheet by division, and then the Commissioner tries the case. Also when a civilian has a complaint against a constable, he hears it. Evidence is never taken on oath; it is more a court of justice than a court of law. And then the presiding officer, whoever he may be adjudicates on the case—fines the man or dismisses him, as the case may be.

140. In fact, the Commissioner or Assistant Commissioner is the sole judge. He decides the case just as a colonel?—Exactly the same.

141. Mr. O'Reilly.—And that extends up to the highest crime, up to dismissal?—Yes.

142. Lord Monck.—Now, is there any different treatment in that respect between the superior officers of the force and the constables. I mean to say, suppose a charge is made against a superintendent, how would that be done?—Exactly the same.

143. Do you consider any dissatisfaction exists in the force at that mode of administering discipline?—On the contrary, I think it is highly satisfactory. I have never heard a complaint yet. The only complaint is what I have seen in the papers, when it was brought before the House of Commons that I dismissed two men and gave no reason for it, and that is that the Commissioner ought not to have the power of dismissing the men without giving them a reason.

144. Mr. Blackwood.—I suppose if a civilian has a charge against a police constable, he may bring it in the police courts?—If he is not satisfied with my decision. If a case is brought before me by a civilian of a police constable having ill-treated him—knocked him on the head and hurt him, I consider it is one that should be dealt with by one of the divisional magistrates; and I give the name, number, and residence of the constable to the civilian, and tell him to take it before the magistrate—I afford him every assistance.

145. Lord Monck.—In fact he would be punished as a member of society?—Yes.

146. And you would dismiss him for having acted wrongly as a policeman?—Yes, dismissal is the highest punishment I can inflict. I don't think that is sufficient for a man who ill-treats another in the street.

147. In the first instance, perhaps you would tell us what is the extent of the district which is supervised by your officers—I mean the city of Dublin, of course, and how far around the city of Dublin?—As nearly as I can recollect, thirty square miles.

148. It extends to Ballybrack?—Yes, and extends to Chapelizod and Inchicore.

149. How far in the southerly and northern directions?—To Milltown, and in the other direction to Ballybough-bridge, on the road to Clontarf; in fact an area of about thirty square miles; the farthest point I have is Ballybrack, the entrance to Ballybrack, Killiney.

150. What is the precise number of men?—At this instant I have not got more than 450 men on street duty altogether.

151. But that is not the nominal strength?—That is the present strength; the nominal strength is 845 constables.

152. You have not got your establishment?—No, I have not.

153. You don't consider your present number is sufficient for your purpose?—No, I don't think it is, for this reason that it has been very much interfered with by calls in various directions.

154. How long is it since the establishment of 860 men, or whatever the number is, was fixed?—I don't know whether it was increased from the first. It was in 1837 when the police force was established first, and I don't know whether it has been increased since or not.

155. Has it been increased in your time?—It has been increased by twenty supernumeraries during the Fenian times. I was allowed to have twenty supernumeraries, and then I applied to get twenty more—forty.

156. Has that number been kept on the establishment?—It has; I have often had that.

157. But your fixed establishment has never been increased?—No, never in my time.

158. Then you are prepared at all events to state that even if you had a full establishment you have not a man too many?—Indeed I have not.

159. Do you think you have too few?—I think I have too few men.

160. What do you think the increase ought to be?—I think if I had 300 more men, I need not increase the officers. If I had 200 more constables I think it would make the force much more efficient. Will you allow me to explain that there are a number of men employed on special duty who come out of that 800; for instance, there are eighteen men in the Exhibition, which makes a great hole; then there are a certain number of men employed in the Four Courts, and in various places of that sort, paid for, and you see these take away from the strength of the force.

161. Could you hand in a table showing the population whom this establishment was fixed, and the increase that has taken place since that period?—Yes.*

162. Mr. O'Reilly.—And perhaps you could give the number of men on special service that are paid for?—Yes, I have all that, but I had better send it in all together. (See No. III. in Appendix.)

163. Mr. Blackwood.—What do you consider to be the test of the insufficiency of the force?—The constant complaints of civilians that they cannot find constables when they want them.

164. Do you consider the men overworked?—No. I don't think they complain of being overworked; they are much more overworked now than formerly; they complain, not as regards hours—they have the same number of hours—but that they have more to direct their attention to.

165. Lord Monck.—The existence of so large a rural area within your jurisdiction inflicts a considerable additional labour?—Very great additional labour; for instance, I have no station nearer Killiney and Ballybrack than Dalkey, which is nearly three miles from them. The constables have to go out to these places on their beats, and must come back again; if they take a prisoner at Ballybrack they are obliged to bring that prisoner to Dalkey, and deliver their charge. The consequence is that the people of Killiney complain bitterly. I have had memorials from them, stating that they pay the same police rate as other people, eight pence in the pound, and they think it very bad they never see a policeman.

166. Would it be possible, with a view to economise the expense of the service, to throw out of your district some of those outlying country places, and put them under the Constabulary, so as to concentrate your force?—I have always been of opinion that the Constabulary might do the Phœnix Park, which is a large area. I have to do that. They have a depot in the Phœnix Park, and a barracks there, and I think if the Park were taken in it would be an advantage.

167. Mr. O'Reilly.—Is it not the case that the central government pays the whole cost of the Constabulary, while the locality pays 8d. in the pound for your force?—Exactly.

* See reply to question 557.

C

October 22.

Colonel Henry
Atwell Lake,
C.B.

168. And possibly the Government would be very reluctant to increase the duties of the Constabulary, whom they have to pay, in order to exempt Killiney and these places from the payment of 8d. in the pound?—Yes; his lordship asked me the question, and I was not speaking for myself.

169. Mr. BLACKWOOD.—I suppose the area over which the Metropolitan Police act is fixed by the city boundaries and the area which pays city rates?—That is so.

170. Lord MONCK.—Do you wish to add anything to your evidence?—I don't know whether this is the proper time to mention it, but I have got a memorial from the Assistant Commissioner. He complains that his salary is too small for the position which he holds—that he thinks it was regulated by that of the police magistrates—the divisional magistrates, who had then only £600, a year, and they have been increased to £800, and the chief magistrate to £900; and he only gets £600 a year. Taking into consideration the arduous and varied duties the Assistant Commissioner has to perform, and comparing his salary with that of an officer of police of similar position in other police forces, I cannot but consider that Captain Talbot has just grounds for applying to have his salary increased, either by actual pay or by allowances, as the Commissioners may see fit. Each of the Assistant Commissioners in London draws £800 a year, with allowances, making up their annual salary to upwards of £1,200 a year. I may add that Captain Talbot is a most zealous and efficient officer, and conducts his duties to my entire satisfaction. Under all the circumstances of the case, I trust the Commissioners may be pleased to consider his application favourably. (*See* A in Appendix IV.)

171. Mr. BLACKWOOD.—Is he one of the magistrates?—I am speaking of my Assistant Commissioner. I don't know whether it is proper for me to mention—but perhaps you would excuse my doing so—a matter personal to myself, which I do reluctantly. I allude to the horse allowance which I draw, and which I represented to the Government very frequently; but it has never been remedied yet. I am obliged to keep a horse to visit all the out stations and barracks, and places of that sort; and if there is any disturbance in the city, it is necessary for me to be mounted. It is fully recognised that I am obliged to keep a horse, and the Assistant Commissioner the same. I am allowed £40 a year for the horse. It is totally insufficient for the purpose.

172. Do you include in that the cost of the groom?—That is the whole amount that is allowed for groom and everything. If I may be allowed to remark, my superintendents draw more; they draw £70 odd. The Commissioner of London draws, I think, £83, and a great many other officers who are obliged to keep a horse.

173. Lord MONCK.—Do you know what the regulation allowance is in the army?—Two shillings a day; but they also have a soldier servant, which I have not.

174. Is there any other statement you would like to put before the Commissioners?—No; I think not, unless I might be permitted to say a few words with regard to my own salary. It was fixed at its present amount by Act of Parliament in 1859, when the necessaries of life, as well as house-rent, were far more reasonable than at present. Perhaps I may be allowed to observe that both the Assistant Commissioners of Police in London, and the Head Constable of Liverpool, draw, including their allowances, a higher rate of pay than I do as Chief Commissioner. I think I may safely say that my position is one of far greater responsibility, if not of actual labour; but I confidently leave my case in the hands of the Commissioners, and will not trouble them with any further observations on a subject so entirely personal.

175. What staff have you got in your office in the Castle?—I mean in the way of clerks—and how is

it composed?—There is a gentleman called the accountant; then there is the chief financial clerk; there is a registrar of carriages; there are three clerks under the accountant, and two clerks under the registrar of carriages.

176. Five clerks in all?—I think that is all.

177. Mr. BLACKWOOD.—And the surgeon and apothecary?—Yes.

178. Lord MONCK.—Have you sufficient occupation for the clerks?—Yes; I think they are very well occupied.

179. Mr. BLACKWOOD.—As regards salary I see the accountant gets £350, rising by £20 to £500?—To £500.

180. The registrar of carriages gets £210, rising by £10 to £320; the finance clerk the same, and the junior clerks £90, rising by £10 to £200?—That is so.

181. Do you think the salaries of the accountant, the registrar, and the clerks are sufficient?—For a series of years they have been complaining. I suppose there is no body of gentlemen who have complained so much of their salaries as those in the Constabulary of Police office. Some of the senior clerks have been a long while in the service, and they state their complaints very fully.

182. Are the five clerks in your office junior clerks?—Yes; my observation applies more to the three under the accountant, who asked me to bring their case forward. I don't know whether that comes under the Civil Service Staff.*

183. What are the hours of attendance?—They come in at ten and leave at four; but very often they are kept a great deal later, as it depends on the amount of work. The accountant and finance clerks have very hard work indeed.

184. What leave do they have?—When they ask leave I give it to them according to the time I consider I can spare them; sometimes they get a month or three weeks in the year.

185. Lord MONCK.—Not more than that?—I think there have been certain cases in which they have got more.

186. As a rule?—There is not any rule; it depends so very much on the amount of work that is going on.

187. Mr. O'REILLY.—Are any of these clerks in the position of policemen?—No; with the exception of one man who had been a policeman years ago.

188. Could not you find men in your own force capable of doing clerks' work. I suppose it is not very high class work?—I might find men no doubt, but these men are not appointed by me.

189. I am asking could you not find these men in the force?—I could.

190. And wouldn't they be glad to get the position?—Very glad indeed.

191. To get the position and something like good pay?—With the exception of the accountant and the financial clerk.

192. You could not get men of that stamp?—And perhaps the assistant to the financial clerk, who is a very clever man.

193. With the exception of these, you could provide the men?—Yes; the only thing is when the accountant is away. I would have a difficulty in supplying his place.

194. But, as I take it, your view is that the accountant and finance clerk must be men of a superior class?—Oh, yes, of a very superior class indeed.

195. Would it not be possible to have one or other of these always present?—That is the way I do now.

196. And then with regard to the other clerks, are there not men of your force to whom it would be promotion and a very desirable reward for service to be promoted to the position of clerks?—Yes, it would; there is one clerk under the financial clerk, and two under the accountant; the accountant acts as secretary.

197. Lord MONCK.—Would these clerks be re-

quired to be of a superior class?—The financial clerks would; there are two other clerks besides these, and their places I could supply out of the force.

198. Mr. O'REILLY.—And then there are three connected with the carriage department?—Yes

199. And could you not supply these also?—No, I don't think it would be easy to supply these; the truth is it is a very important position.

200. Is it more important than one of your inspectors or superintendents?—Oh, no.

201. Mr. BLACKWOOD.—I suppose you feel that although one or two of the places of the second-class clerks could be filled by men from the police force, the others ought still to be filled by men of a different stamp in order to become qualified to fill the posts of accountant and financial clerk eventually, and so have a succession of men qualifying for the higher post?—Exactly.

202. Lord MONCK.—I understand you to say, with reference to the future, that it might be possible, consistently, with the efficiency of the office, to make four out of the five clerks writers, and give the positions as rewards to deserving men of the service? I think so, certainly.

203. Mr. BLACKWOOD.—Which of the clerks in your office do you consider have any just ground of complaint with regard to pay?—The accountant would be very glad to arrive at his maximum, and I think that he deserves it; it is a very important post; he gets £400 I think.

204. Pardon me, the accountant begins at £350

and goes on to £500. It is now only £370, which would imply that he has been only one year in that position. The finance clerk is at his maximum?—Is he?

205. Yes, he is at £320, which is the maximum of that grade?—It is the other two clerks under the accountant who make the most complaints.

206. Lord MONCK.—What are the duties of the finance clerk?—He has the whole of the financial department, under the direction of the accountant, he keeps and prepares all the accounts for the Audit Office, Treasury, &c., and every single thing that comes under the finance department goes through him for recording in the books, and for the preparation of the accounts.

207. Then the accountant is a secretary?—He is a secretary; I don't know the reason why they call him an accountant; some few years ago there was a secretary, an accountant, and I forget what the other was called, and all the offices were united into one, and he was called the accountant.

208. And had you a finance clerk as well then?—Yes, we had under the Receiver; he wasn't called finance clerk, he was called chief clerk in the receiver's office.

209. How long is it since that arrangement was made?—It was in consequence of the Act of Parliament of 1859, which abolished the joint commission, and all the provisions of that Act were carried out immediately after with the exception of the joint commission, which went on until September of last year; it was in the year 1860.

Superintendent Richard Corr examined.

210. Lord MONCK.—What position do you hold in the Dublin Metropolitan Police?—A Divisional Superintendent

211. We have heard at very considerable length from Colonel Lake, a general statement of the grievances of the force, and we have also received from him the memorial of the men, and we are anxious to hear from you, as one of the officers of that body, if you have anything further to add. Would you tell us, in your rank in the force, if you have any complaint to make as to your position. We have already gone over the comparative rates of pay. Have you anything to add to what has been already stated?—The present dearness of provisions presses heavily on every member in the force. I may mention that I joined the service on the 1st of December, 1837, so that I am thirty-five years in the force next December. At that time I could buy the best beef in the city for 3½d. a pound; mutton was about the same price; and potatoes were only 2d a stone—now they are something like 1s. and 1s. 2d. With regard to the married men in the service, they are, in fact, in a state of misery. I know the case of a married man, with four or five children, and his wife, all of whom live in one room; and he pays 3s. 6d. or 4s. for that room, which they all occupy.

212. A week?—A week. He has cooking and washing, in the shape of coal, to pay for. Well, he comes off duty at six o'clock, and retires to bed in the same room where his wife and children are, and he cannot get that refreshing sleep that he would require for his night's duty; and he pays 4s. a week rent, and 3s. 6d. or 2s. 8d. a week for coal. Take that out of the pay of a first rate constable, and it will leave him about 12s. 6d. to support himself and his family.

213. I may tell you that we are very fully informed on this point. We have gone into the whole question of pay, grievances, and such matters. What we want to know is, whether in your special rank there is any particular grievance of which you have to complain?—As regards the pay, I may say that I have thirteen children, my wife, and two servants, to support on £310 a year.

214. On the question of pay, which we perfectly understand, I see that this memorial, which came from

your force, states that the superintendents of the force have to purchase their own uniforms. Is that so?—It is.

215. Do you consider that a grievance?—I do consider that a grievance.

216. In fact, as far as I can gather from this memorial, the members of the force of your rank complain of having to contribute to the expense of purchasing their uniform, and of the inadequacy of allowance for their office?—Yes; I do not think any member of my rank has any further cause of complaint.

217. What are the perquisites you speak of here? You say, "allowance granted for rent of office and perquisites should be increased?"—There is £35 given to a superintendent who is not furnished with quarters; the office is altogether too small.

218. You say that it should be increased to a reasonable amount. What would you consider a reasonable amount?—I would consider £40 a reasonable amount for a superintendent not supplied with quarters.

219. Mr. O'REILLY.—That would enable him to keep his office, and supply him with a house?—No, it would not.

220. It would not?—No, it would not; I paid £40 a year for a house.

221. You paid £40 a year for a house?—Yes.

222. Now would you tell me where it was you were paying that rent?—No. 3, Upper Buckingham-street. I was allowed £25 for an office.

223. Could you tell us how many rooms that house had?—Eight rooms.

224. Were there any other apartments in it?—There were eight rooms, besides a front and back kitchen and a stable; I paid £40 a year for a ten-roomed house, with a coach-house and stable for one horse.

225. Lord MONCK.—When did you last pay it?—we want to know if there is any change?—On the 1st of August I paid the last rent.

226. This year?—Yes.

227. Mr. O'REILLY.—When were you changed?—About three months ago I was changed from the C to the B Division, and I have got quarters in the Lower Castle Yard since—I have got them free.

228. Mr. BLACKWOOD.—What allowance do you get

C 2

October 22.
Superintendent
Richard Corr.

—I get an allowance of 2s. a day for a man-servant, 2s. a day for a horse, half a ton of coal for the office in the winter, and a quarter of a ton in the summer months.

229. Mr. O'REILLY.—A week?—A month; that is a small allowance.

230. Lord MONCK.—How long have you been superintendent of the Dublin Metropolitan Police?—I was promoted to the position of superintendent on the 1st of April, 1863. That is nine years last April.

231. As I understand you, with regard to your own rank in the service, you think an increase of pay, to put you on an equality with the same force in England, would satisfy you?—Just so; an increased sum of pay, and a somewhat increased allowance for house-rent, are all we want. That is all we require; we would be perfectly satisfied with that.

232. With regard to the system of promotion in the service, from your knowledge of the force, which must be considerable, do you think it gives satisfaction to the men, on the whole?—Nothing can be more so; of course the promotion in the service is dependent on the Chief Commissioner and the Assistant Commissioner, to promote the deserving men best entitled to it, and no better or more unbiased man could be found than the present Commissioner.

233. Your answer equally applies as to punishments in your force—the punitive administration of the force?—Perfectly so.

234. They are perfectly satisfied with the discipline carried on in the force?—No doubt of it.

235. You do not make any complaint of the system of discipline, or the organization of the force?—Not the slightest.

236. Your complaint has only reference to the remuneration of the force?—I do not think any man in the service has a shadow of complaint, on any other ground. I joined the service on its formation, when it was 1,200 strong, and there is not one of those serving in it at present but myself, which shows the severity of the service.

237. Have you any fault to find with the systems of pensions?—Yes; with regard to the pension, and

the superannuation allowance. I may state that after my long period of service now, if I was taken suddenly ill, and if, for the benefit of my family, I would prefer to get a gratuity to a pension, all I could receive would be fifteen years' gratuity.

238. What do you mean?—All I could get would be a gratuity of fifteen years. That is, all I would get would be a month's pay for each year for fifteen years.

239. You don't mean that you would be entitled to fifteen years' pay?—No; only to a month's pay for fifteen years, or in other words to fifteen months' pay after my long service.

240. Mr. O'REILLY.—If you gave up your pension?—If I gave up my pension, if I was taken dangerously ill, and that I thought it better, for the benefit of my family, to receive a gratuity, instead of a pension, all I should be entitled to would be fifteen years' gratuity.

241. Lord MONCK.—Is there anything else you would like to tell us, in connexion with the grievances of the force? We have already gone very fully into the matter with Colonel Lake?—Well, I think, if in each district there was a plot of ground procured, on which was built a range of cottages for the married men of the division, it would be a grand thing, it would be a great benefit to the married men, and do good to the service at large, inasmuch as it would afford ample accommodation for them. Let the men have them at a moderate rent, and in a few years they would pay all the expense entailed on their outlay, so as not to have them living, as at present, in the lanes and alleys of the city.

242. Now, as I understand, the married men are living in the lanes and alleys of the city, the only restriction being that they should live within their division?—Yes.

243. Mr. BLACKWOOD.—Are all the unmarried men living in barrack?—They are.

244. As I understand, there is no complaint from the unmarried men, with regard to the stoppage for the rations for their dinners?—No; there is not—they are quite content.

Inspector John
Mallon.

Inspector John Mallon examined.

245. Lord MONCK.—What is your position in the Dublin Metropolitan Police?—I am an Inspector in the Detective Department.

246. An inspector, I believe, is the next grade to sergeant?—No, it is a grade higher; there is the position of acting inspector between sergeant and inspector.

247. Mr. O'REILLY.—I take it that the position of acting inspector is the next grade to inspector?—Yes.

248. Lord MONCK.—I may inform you that we have gone very carefully into the whole case of the Dublin Metropolitan Police with Colonel Lake; he stated that he represented the feelings of the men of the force, as regards their grievances, which have been put forward in their memorial—is that your opinion?—That is my opinion.

249. We should like to hear from you, whether in your own special rank there is any special grievance of which you have to complain?—We think the pay inadequate.

250. Mr. O'REILLY.—We have gone through that question very fully already?—Well, I may state that in the detective department the men do duty in plain clothes, and their duties are of a more disagreeable character than the duties of the men on ordinary police duty—for instance, a detective requires more tact than the ordinary man, as he is obliged to deal with and encounter persons who commit crimes, whose detection is more or less difficult. We apply ourselves to the detection of crime—of serious crime. Besides that, we have the supervision of convicts who are released on licence; the supervision of persons who reside in the Metropolitan Police dis-

trict who are discharged from prison, subject to police supervision under the Prevention of Crimes Act of 1871. We have the supervision of pawn offices, and the supervision of all public vehicles, and of the drivers and conductors is attached to the detective department. The only complaint with us is the want of sufficient pay.

251. Lord MONCK.—That seems to be a complaint that runs through the whole force. You do not complain of the discipline?—No.

252. Nor of your promotion?—No; I only speak of our department—they complain of want of pay.

253. Your men complain of inadequacy of pay and want of an additional allowance in respect of clothes?—Yes; for instance, a first-class constable has only 20s. a week; he has only 1s. a week more than the ordinary constable, although he is obliged to appear in respectable plain clothes upon all occasions.

254. Mr. O'REILLY.—Then he has an allowance of 5s. for clothes?—No, there is no allowance in the detective department in lieu of clothes.

255. Then that is done away with?—It is done away with since 1859, but when a judge or magistrate makes a remark, recommending a detective to the consideration of Commissioners, and when the detective has proved himself efficient, as shown by the discharge of his duties throughout the year, the Commissioners may give him a reward of £1 or 10s. for the remark of the judge or magistrate. On an average, on the whole year round, it may be about £2 10s.

256. That would not buy a suit of clothes?—Not at all.

257. Then, in point of fact, you have no allowance for clothes?—No, we have not.

258. But you are supplied with a suit of uniform?—One suit.

259. How often?—Perhaps once in seven years, and then only when it is too seedy to appear in court.

260. And, therefore, the public gains the price of a uniform on you every year?—Yes, they do.

261. Lord Monck.—For which they pay only 1s. more than to an ordinary constable?—Yes.

262. Mr. O'Reilly.—Do you know the cost of a uniform?—No, I have no idea of the cost.* There is one thing that would entitle the men of the Detective Department to some consideration, and that is, in endeavouring to catch thieves, and in the detection of crime, they must incur expense, so that the difference between their pay and that of a constable's uniform would not be sufficient.

263. There is nothing else which you wish to state?—There is no special grievance, beyond what I state, want of pay.

October 22.

Inspector John Mallon.

Thomas Gaffney examined.

Thomas Gaffney.

264. Lord Monck.—What position do you hold in the Dublin Metropolitan Police?—That of an Inspector.

265. Well, I may tell you, that we have had Colonel Lake here this morning, and we have gone very fully into the grievances of the force, which appear to him to resolve themselves into a question of pay and allowances, and we have before us the memorial which Colonel Lake presented. Now, we wish to ascertain from you, whether, in your rank, there is any special grievance which you wish to bring before us?—None whatever, except inadequacy of pay.

266. A little more money?—Quite so.

267. Mr. O'Reilly.—What is your present rate of pay?—£133 a year—I belong to the first class. I am the senior Inspector of the service now.

268. You provide your own uniform?—I provide my own uniform, boots, and everything—it is quite too much for me latterly.

269. Lord Monck.—How long have you been in the service?—Nearly twenty-six years.

270. Have you any complaint to make with regard to the administration, promotions, punishments of the force, or anything of that sort?—Not the least; we have implicit faith in the Chief Commissioner and his assistant, and we have nothing to complain of, on the score of promotion or discipline.

271. Is there any feeling of complaint with regard to the pensions?—Latterly, we are not getting as good a class of men as we did formerly, and I believe that that is accounted for by the small allowance granted on retiring from the force, and other things. When they retire their constitution is shattered, after what they have to go through, being frequently assaulted. In this country the position of a constable is anything but an enviable one.

272. You spoke of not getting a good class of recruits; do you think if the pay of the force were increased, that that would have the effect of restoring the former state of things, as to recruiting?—I think so.

273. You are aware that the pension granted is regulated by Act of Parliament, and if the pay were increased the pension would also as a matter of course be increased?—I am quite aware of that.

274. Mr. Blackwood.— Did any of the men, to your knowledge, who resigned, enlist in the English force—go into the London Metropolitan Police?—Oh, a great many did so, a great many that resigned here did go into the London Police.

275. Mr. O'Reilly.—Did any of them go to the City of London Police Force?—I think some of them did, and some went to the police forces of other cities in England.

276. Mr. Blackwood.—I suppose that many of them, being Irishmen, would be willing to remain in the Dublin Metropolitan Police Force, even although the pay was not exactly equal to the pay they would receive in the London Police, in consideration of being in their own country?—They consider the necessaries of life quite as high here as in London, and certainly I have no doubt they all think you will be good enough to allow them to draw the same pay.

277. Mr. O'Reilly.—The men now supply their own boots?—They do.

278. Would they consider it an advantage to be enabled to get boots from the Government store at a contract price?—I do not think it would be an advantage to them to do so, because they are always astir and walk a great deal, and if the boots do not properly fit the men, they get knocked up, but if the men are properly fitted, they are able to walk more, and do more active duty. I think they would prefer being allowed the cash with which to procure them.

279. I can quite understand that. Now, with regard to the under-clothing with which the men supply themselves; I see by the prices which the men put down as that which they are obliged to pay, that they are a good deal higher than that which the army is supplied with for good articles. They put down five shillings for a shirt; now would it be a gain to them if they got them out of the Government stores?—I have no moral doubt they would be got cheaper by a contract price.

280. Mr. Blackwood.—The men do not complain of the stoppages for fuel, lodging, or for dinners?—They would rather, of course, those stoppages were not made, but when they have to be made, they think the stoppages are reasonable under the circumstances.

281. Mr. O'Reilly.—Are they satisfied with the messing arrangements for dinner? Do they think they get good value for their money?—They do.

282. They arrange the messing, as I understand amongst themselves?—They do; they almost always elect a man whose duties are lessened that he may attend to that alone.

283. Is there any regulation as to the quantity of meat each man receives?—The messman generally gets 1 lb. of meat for each man for his dinner.

284. Do you know how long the messing charge has been the same—5s. 6d. a week?—I cannot say exactly.

285. I mean is it a great many years?—Oh, not a great many years.

286. Was it less formerly?—Much less.

287. The messing charge?—Much less.

288. Could you ascertain for us what the messing charge was formerly in the force?—There would be a difficulty in that; we did not get into the system of messing until, comparatively speaking, recently.

289. Mr. Blackwood.—Now, with regard to the stoppages from the men's pay on the sick list, it is urged by the members of the force that no stoppages should be made. You must have much experience as to the discipline of the force, having been so long in it: what do you think the effect would be if no stoppages were made—would it lead to many pretending to be sick who were not in reality sick?—In some instances it might have that tendency, but as a general rule there is no time that a man requires the whole of his pay more than when he is sick; the doctor ought to be a good judge as to whether he is sick or not.

290. Mr. O'Reilly.—Is a man's pay who is put on the sick list generally stopped if he is ill?—Not generally; there are instances in which the whole of the pay is allowed him.

291. Lord Monck.—With regard to that Colonel Lake exercises his discretion?—He does, my lord, and I do not think I ever heard a murmur as to the exercise of that discretion.

---

* Information given in answer to Question 576.

Richard Manly examined.

292. Lord MONCK.—What position do you hold in the Dublin Metropolitan Police?—Acting Inspector.

293. The last witness we examined was an inspector?—An inspector.

294. Then you are in the rank between a sergeant and an inspector?—Yes.

295. Well, we desire to hear the grievances of the force, and we are anxious to learn them truly, and to get at the bottom of them. We had Colonel Lake before us, and he went very fully into the question of pay, and gave us all the information he could on that subject. We should like to know from you whether there is any special grievance in your particular rank you wish to bring before us?—I don't know of any.

296. The whole question is one of pay?—Yes.

297. You have no complaint to make as to the administration of the force, the promotion, punishment, or anything of that kind?—I have no complaint to make of the duty at all.

298. In fact, you have nothing to tell us beyond, I believe, what Colonel Lake laid before us, us to the feelings of the force with respect to certain grievances and your memorial?—No, I have nothing further to say.

William Thorpe examined.

299. Lord MONCK.—What position do you hold in the Dublin Metropolitan Police Force?—Sergeant.

300. How long have you been sergeant?—A year and eight months.

301. How long have you been in the force?—Fifteen years.

302. Well, we have heard all your complaints, which Colonel Lake laid before us, with regard to the rate of pay, and other matters of that kind, and we are anxious to know whether you in your grade have any special complaint to make, and any special grievance to bring before us?—The only grievance we have is the inadequacy of pay.

303. You have no complaint to make on behalf of the force as to the system of promotion, punishment, &c.?—The system of promotion is carried out on a principle of justice to every man.

304. Is there any complaint about the question of pensions?—Yes, the men joining of late years think the pension does not offer a sufficient inducement for them to remain in the service.

305. Taking into account that the London Metropolitan Police are pensioned on the same scale, and that a great many go to London in consequence of the inducement of higher pay, if the pay was somewhat more equalised, do you think they would remain here?—I think not. Some of the men have gone to London, and they have written back to us to say that the people there are not so rough or hostile as those we have to do with here.

306. Independent of the question of pay, you think they would have gone to London?—They would, from the reason I have stated.

307. So that is the account you have received from those who left?—Yes; we have all comrades there, and they have written to say that they prefer to be there, as the people are not so hostile to the police as they are here.

308. Now, do you think that hostility has grown up lately or was it always so?—No; not always—within the last four or five years.

309. Mr. O'REILLY.—Have you any comrades in the City of London Police?—Yes. I have a brother.

310. And there are some men whom you know in the London Metropolitan Police?—It is in the London Metropolitan Police my brother is.

311. Then you don't know anybody in the City of London Police?—No; I do not.

Samuel Cowan examined.

312. Lord MONCK.—What position do you hold in the Dublin Metropolitan Police Force?—Acting-sergeant.

313. How long have you been in the force?—Twelve years.

314. Well, we have heard from Colonel Lake, who appears to represent the feelings of the force very fairly and very fully, the complaints as to the rates of pay, and we also heard from the different grades what they had to say. Have you anything to add to his statement? We have got your memorial and we wish to know if you have anything to add to what is there set forth?—We have no other special grievance at all, except the inadequacy of the pay.

315. That is your sole cause of complaint?—That is our sole cause of complaint; I can show you that I could not live on my present scale of pay, which is 20s. a week; out of that I have to pay 1s. 6d. a week, rent; coals, 2s. 6d.; bread, 5s. 4d.; tea and sugar, 2s. 6d.; milk, 1s. 2d.; besides potatoes, &c., not to mention meat or fish. I have a wife and three children to support.

316. Mr. BLACKWOOD.—I see the lower grade of acting-sergeant gets the same rate of pay as the highest rate of constables, £1 a week—did you get that rate of pay when a constable?—No, I had only 19s.; a first-class constable gets 19s., and an acting-sergeant only gets 1s. of an increase.

317. Then there is an increase?—There is an increase of 1s. a week for the acting-sergeant—there is 1s. difference between the two ranks.

318. Lord MONCK.—Is there any other observation that you would like to make to us?—There is not.

319. Why was it you came here to give evidence—were you sent by the office, or were you delegated by the men?—I was delegated by the men.

320. That is, you came here to represent the men of your own rank?—I came to represent the men of my own rank.

321. And with Colonel Lake's full approbation?—With Colonel Lake's full approbation.

James Curran examined.

322. Lord MONCK.—What position do you hold in the force?—First-rate constable.

323. What is your pay?—Nineteen shillings a week.

324. How long have you been in the force?—I will be, I think, nine years next April.

325. We wish to know, independent of the question of pay whether you have any cause of complaint of the service, or whether you know of any cause of complaint amongst the men; I may tell you that we have had fully from Colonel Lake everything as to the pay and allowances?—Do you mean married men and single men?

326. Mr. O'REILLY.—Yes?—There is only one question about which there is any complaining, and that is as to the competition for the rank of sergeant from constable, and as to the re-distribution of the different rates; the rates are all very unfairly divided.

327. Lord MONCK.—What is your idea about the

competition for the rank of acting-sergeant—how is it carried on, first?—Every man going up for examination for acting-sergeant must be a first-rate man. They are examined in Kevin-street, and there is a list of approved candidates one after the other published. That list stands good until it is exhausted, sometimes for one year or two years, and sometimes the list will stand five years before it is exhausted, and then a man promoted to the rank of a first-rate constable the day after that examination is debarred from all chance of promotion until that list is exhausted. The majority of the men would wish that there should be certain marks given by the officers for efficiency and good conduct. They think it should be examiners outside of the force, like the Civil Service examinations, but upon an humble scale, and that so many should not be put on the list to throw out men so long in the service.

328. What I understand from you is this, that when vacancies occur, there should be a new examination, and that the best man should be selected, and the old lists, from former examinations, set aside?—Yes; the last time we had an examination there were about forty-five put on the list; shortly after that there were four more; in about a week there was another lot; there were about forty next, which brought it up to nearly 100. We knew that there were many on the list who should not be officers at all. They would have to improve in every way. What we ask is, that the lists should be made shorter—that they should be annual. I do not mean to say that the old lists should be set aside.

329. Mr. O'REILLY.—What you would like would be an annual examination which would be open to all the men joining?—Yes, to the men of the first rate; the men of the lower rates do not expect it.

330. But the present system, in fact, amounts to promotion by seniority, provided that the men come up to a certain standard?—Well, I take it to be that.

331. What you would wish would be to see it carried on by competition among all the qualified men in the next rank below?—Yes, and if a man is not fit, leave him where he was.

332. Would not that create a good deal of discontent amongst the men, to see a clever and younger man promoted over their heads?—That might be so, but on the other hand, the spirit of emulation would be such that each would improve himself to press for the next examination. I do not mean that they should go from rank to rank, but merely for the first rank. With regard to the rates, I may tell you that there are four rates of constables. Before the last commission there were only three rates, and at that time there was a class of constables who got good service pay for over five years' service. In the second scale we usually got 1s. 2d. a week for what was called good service pay. That good service pay was done away with There happened to be 118 men of the second class on the good service pay, and they were made a rate for themselves. We then had a first and second rate, and the ordinary second class and third class, and then a fourth class was made.

333. Do you mean that there are four classes of constables?—Yes, there are.

334. Besides the supernumeraries?—Besides the supernumeraries; the supernumeraries in the depôt do not count at all.

335. Mr. BLACKWOOD.—What are the different rates of pay?—Well, the first rate is 19s. a week; the second rate is 17s. 6d.; the third rate is 16s. 9d., and the fourth rate, I think, is 16s. 6d.

336. Lord MONCK.—We understand that those are the two suggestions you would make with regard to promotion and re-distribution of the rates?—Yes, my lord; I believe that there are 350 constables on the first rate. Now, before you attain to that, a man runs the chance that he must have nine years' service. The second rate is 118 at present, which runs up to six years' service, and there is the third rate which is 350, who attain it in three or four months, and remain at that for six years. If the second rate was proportionably increased from the third, it would be more equalized with the others, and give equal promotion to a number of men. The rates should be more fairly and evenly divided.

337. I presume that you were sent here to represent the men?—I was sent to represent the constables of my own division, and with me is one from each of the other divisions, and I was chosen out of the six representatives of the six divisions to attend and give evidence here.

Adjourned.

October 22.
James Curren

OCTOBER 23, 1872.

Francis Hinds, esq., examined.

October 23.
Francis Hinds,
esq.

338. Lord MONCK.—What position do you occupy?—I am Secretary and Accountant to the Metropolitan Police.

339. You are called accountant, but I believe your duties are principally those of secretary?—Secretary, and accountant also.

340. You are responsible for the accounts?—Responsible for the accounts; for the expenditure of the establishment.

341. I see that your office consists of an accountant, a finance clerk, and a registrar of carriages?—Yes.

342. And five second-class clerks?—Yes.

343. Now, how are these five second-class clerks distributed? What are their duties?—Well, there are two clerks employed assisting the registrar of carriages in preparing carriage licenses, issuing carriage licenses, and receiving carriage rents and publicans' license fees.

344. They receive rents?—Yes; at times of pressure. The carriage rent is collected annually for a certain class of vehicles, half-yearly for another class, when the carmen come to the office to pay the amount to the registrar and to these clerks.

345. Mr. O'REILLY.—In presence of the registrar?—Yes; in fact the object of the clerks in receiving money is to assist the registrar, the crowd in the office being very great at the payment periods.

346. Lord MONCK.—The registrar is responsible?—Yes.

347. Two of the clerks act under him?—Yes. One clerk is employed in the finance office, where the pensions are paid monthly and quarterly, and when not employed there he is employed in the secretary's office. The other two clerks are employed permanently in the secretary's office. One is employed in copying and writing letters, the other assists him, checks the accounts of the department, and makes out pensions, gratuities, pay lists, &c.

348. Checks the accounts?—Yes; the accounts come in from the several police divisions, and they are checked there and sent up for payment to the finance department.

349. Then the finance clerk does not exercise any check?—Well, accounts, bills, &c., go in the first instance to the finance office and are checked there, and then they come down stairs where they are again checked in the Commissioner's office.

350. Mr. O'REILLY.—What do you mean by the Commissioner's office? I have the secretary's office, and the registrar of carriages, and the finance department. What is the Commissioner's office?—We often understand the Commissioner's office to be the secretary's office.

351. Lord MONCK.—And the secretary's office is the Commissioner's office?—Yes.

352. It appears all these clerks have more or less to do with checking the accounts?—They have. In

October 23.
Francis Hinds,
esq.

the carriage department as a matter of course they receive money, and are also employed in filling carriage licences, and recording them in the registers, &c.

353. But is not the registrar of carriages responsible for that?—He is responsible for all that.

354. He sees that they do their work?—Yes.

355. And, in point of fact, any man who could read and write and keep accounts would equally well serve his purpose there?—Yes.

356. Mr. O'REILLY.—Who is responsible?—The registrar is responsible, but it would be utterly impossible for one man to receive all the money at the payment periods.

357. What I want to know is this. These two clerks in the registrar of carriages' office appear to me to perform mere mechanical duties?—Yes, to a great extent; but in the absence of the registrar either of the clerks must be competent to take his place.

358. What are the registrar's duties?—He receives and accounts for the money, sees the licences properly filled, and gives information to the public on matters connected with the licensing of public vehicles, and the general business of his office.

359. Is that a duty that goes on continuously all the year round?—Well, licences are filled all the year round, but a more important duty occurs at intervals.

360. At what intervals?—About twice—half-yearly. The carriage duty is received twice—half-yearly. Hackney cars pay £3 annually for their licence, received in two half-yearly sums, the first in February, and the second in July; cabriolets pay £1 4s yearly, in February. Licences are being issued occasionally all the year round.

361. Lord MONCK.—That is small work. You have not more than one or two in the day?—Sometimes half a dozen.

362. But taking the average of the year you would not have work for one man?—Well, probably an hour or two hours a day would do. The carmen are continually losing their badges, and getting new badges and new licences, and new licences have to be prepared annually for all hackney drivers, &c., in Dublin, as renewal licences.

363. Mr. O'REILLY.—They pay for them?—Yes.

364. What are the duties of the finance clerk?—He keeps the books of the department, and prepares the accounts for the Audit Office. He also makes out the accounts of pensions, and pays them monthly and quarterly. He also prepares pawnbrokers' licences, which are sent from his office, with a memorandum from the accountant, to be signed by the magistrate before being issued; further, he prepares Returns for the Treasury, and discharges various other duties in connexion with contracts, stores, &c.

365. What are his clerk's duties?—His duties are to assist the finance clerk, and to be present in the office at the payment of moneys, and to do a good deal of copying.

366. It is not necessary for two men to be present?—It is considered better to have them present.

367. Do you pay generally in cash?—The monthly pensions are paid in cash, and the quarterly payments by cheques on the Bank of Ireland.

368. Now, tell us your own duties, and the clerks connected with you?—My duties are these: I have the conducting of the correspondence of the department, and it is rather voluminous. I have to prepare minutes for the Commissioners on various subjects, abstracts of Acts of Parliament, and orders for the force. Then I sign all the cheques for payment of pensioners and others, and render and am responsible for the accounts prepared for the Audit Office. I also sign the carriage licences, enter into contracts for clothing and other necessaries for the force, and discharge various other duties peculiar to the chief executive officer of the department.

369. Is yours an absolute signature?—No; the Commissioners countersign. No cheque can be paid without my signature and that of one of the Commissioners.

370. Mr. BLACKWOOD.—Are you responsible for the

proper keeping of the account-books of the department?—Well, I am. I hold myself responsible, although I believe that it has been considered that the accountant is not responsible for the keeping of the books.

371. Who is considered responsible?—The books are examined by the Public Accounts Commissioners.

372. But the accountant is to be responsible for the proper keeping of the books?—I see the accounts, and see that the books are properly written up, and have been in the habit of doing so.

373. Were you under the impression, before the recent Treasury minute was issued, that the Public Accounts Commissioners were in any degree responsible for the correctness of the accounts?—Yes.

374. Whence did you get that impression?—The late accountant led me to conclude that I was not exactly responsible for the keeping of the books, but I was responsible for the strict accuracy of the accounts, which I invariably examine with the greatest possible attention to see that every payment is correct, and that there is a voucher for every payment.

375. Which officer of the establishment do you hold responsible for the correct keeping of the books?—We generally look to the finance clerk.

376. Not the Public Accounts Commissioners?—No, but immediately to the department of the Commissioners. There was a feeling that as the Public Accounts Commissioners came here and had the books produced to them, we were relieved from the responsibility of being answerable for them.

377. Were you relieved from the responsibility of the correctness of the books?—No, but the form of the books was prescribed by the Public Accounts Commissioners.

378. I suppose that by the recent Treasury minute the finance clerk would be more properly called by the new title of "clerk in charge of the accounts," since he is the officer who keeps the books and prepares the accounts?—The accounts come down to me monthly, and I check them over and see that there is a voucher for every item, and that the balance in the bank is correct.

379. Have you a technical knowledge of book-keeping yourself?—I have a very good knowledge of book-keeping.

380. But more properly your duties are those of secretary and head of the department under the Commissioners?—Yes; the accounts being a periodical and settled business.

381. Lord MONCK.—You have two clerks under you?—Yes.

382. What are their duties?—Well, one duty is to write and copy letters, and enter letters, and to copy minutes for Government, and to enter those minutes in the Government and other books.

383. In the event of your absence from illness or any other cause, who is to take your place?—The finance clerk is the next senior officer.

384. Mr. O'REILLY.—The work divides itself, I think, in your office into two parts—the correspondence and accounts?—Yes.

385. Now, the accounts are practically kept by the finance clerk?—Yes.

386. I want to know whether you consider the finance clerk responsible for that department, or simply, as your clerk, to keep the accounts?—He is responsible for the accuracy of the books, but I am, as accountant, responsible for the strict accuracy of the accounts and of the books; he is the head of the accountant's branch under the accountant.

387. And you are the accountant, and responsible for that branch?—Yes, I am the accountant, and responsible for that branch; our schedules, which are sent to the paymaster weekly, are all signed by me and countersigned by one of the Commissioners; in fact, nothing can be paid without my signature.

388. The position of finance clerk does not properly speaking include responsibility of the finance, but he is a clerk who is responsible to you for the accuracy of the accounts?—He is responsible to me for the accuracy of the books.

October 28.

Francis Finch, esq.

389. Lord Monck.—In fact no document or account goes through your office to the public under the signature of the finance clerk?—Certainly not.

390. You are the person whose signature authenticates the accuracy of the accounts?—Yes.

391. Mr. O'Reilly.—Would you point out anything in the work of any of those clerks in your office, or in the finance office, or in the office of the registrar of carriages, that requires more in the clerk than a competent knowledge of the English language and a knowledge of accounts?—In the secretary's office some higher knowledge would be required—experience, at all events, of correspondence and of drafting letters, and of preparation of minutes and abstracts.

392. Well, I understood that was your work?—Well, in the event of my absence, there must be some person capable of acting immediately in such a capacity; in fact, it is a rule in all departments that there must be at all events two persons equal to the discharge of a particular duty.

393. Mr. Blackwood.—But the finance clerk would be able to fill your place?—Yes, but he certainly would require the assistance of a senior clerk in the corresponding department, whose duty it is to write letters and assist in the correspondence.

394. Mr O'Reilly.—Yes, but am I right in understanding you that the departments are in fact one?—Yes, in a general practical sense.

395. And all the clerks under you are available for all the work of that department. There is no reason why, in your absence, the finance clerk could not do the correspondence and secretary work of the office, as well as the finance?—Yes, it is one department practically.

396. Mr. Blackwood.—I suppose when you are on leave he occupies your place?—He did so on the last occasion when I was on leave.

397. Don't you think that the duties performed now by clerks might be equally well performed by a well-educated sergeant?—Yes, in every department there must be a great deal of work of a mechanical nature. We have, in times of pressure, called in intelligent constables to our aid.

398. Lord Monck.—The incidental duties of the police force to a certain extent educate them for that kind of work?—Yes; the persons brought in to assist the clerks are constables, and have a good deal of knowledge of the duties of the office.

399. Mr. O'Reilly.—In regard to the registrar of carriages, how far would the superior class of policemen be qualified to discharge the duties of his office?—Well, inasmuch as the registrar must have considerable experience, and as he has charge of large sums of money, it is always very desirable to have the office filled by a responsible person.

400. Do you mean responsible by birth and education, or by being in that position?—Responsible from the position and amount of salary he receives, which should make it worth his while to be a respectable, intelligent person, to take the appointment.

401. But there are no peculiarly intellectual or educational qualifications required in that office?—From the responsibility attached to the office, competency, character, and experience are required by the possessor.

402. Mr. Blackwood.—Do you think that the posts of all five of the clerks, in the event of vacancies occurring, could be filled up by the appointment of either sergeants or constables?—I would rather think that the opinion of the Commissioner is that it would not be desirable to have the five places filled by sergeants or constables. Two of them might be so filled.

403. Lord Monck.—I find that the present registrar is receiving £290 a year?—Yes

404. And that the senior superintendent gets £280 10s. a year?—Yes.

405. So that there is no very important difference between the two. Supposing that the personal qualification of the senior superintendent fitted him for that office is there any reason why he should not occupy it?—None in the least; but I understood the question to refer to sergeants.

406. I have asked you the question in regard to the registrar of carriages, and you say there would be no inconvenience in that, assuming that the qualifications of the man engaged were sufficient. I presume you would not say so of the finance clerk—the requiring special qualifications?—Just so; he should be a first-class accountant and correspondent.

407. Mr. O'Reilly.—Am I right in taking it from you that you think there should be at least one clerk to take your place in case of absence?—Such is my opinion.

408. Lord Monck.—And that there ought to be two men with technical training as clerks in that office?—No doubt.

409. And for the rest you do not see any objection in dealing with them in the way suggested?—None; I see no inconvenience; moderate capacity with some experience being understood.

410. Mr. Blackwood.—The apothecary is an officer of the establishment at a fixed salary?—He is an officer of the establishment at a salary of £50 a year.

411. Is that the only source of his emolument?—It is his only source from the police.

412. Is he entitled to superannuation?—I am not able to answer that question, because the gentleman who at present fills that post is the only one that has ever held the appointment, and the question has never yet been raised; but the medical officer is entitled to superannuation.

413. Lord Monck.—I presume that the apothecary is allowed to conduct his own profession out of doors?—Yes; he has a medical establishment of his own.

414. Mr. O'Reilly.—Do you know does the apothecary supply the medicines?—No; the sum of £50 is granted, and the medicines are supplied by the Apothecaries' Hall. The cost of medicines required does not equal the sum voted by Parliament. The amount expended never comes up to that sum of £50.

415. Mr. Blackwood.—Is there any complaint from the officers of the establishment, including yourself, regarding the rate of salary at present received?—The officers are not at present satisfied with the amount of salary. They look upon their salaries as very inadequate—inadequate as compared with the salaries paid to other departments, and inadequate also in consequence of the increased cost of living and fuel, &c.

416. Lord Monck.—How long is it since the present salaries were fixed?—Not very long; I shall let you know more particularly by referring to the accounts. It is not very long since the Treasury made a small increase, but not the increase asked for.

417. Mr. Blackwood.—With what office in Ireland are you comparing your salaries when you say they are inadequate?—Well, as compared with the Constabulary office, which is almost an analogous establishment; and as compared, also, with the Police Magistrates' office. The maximum salary of our junior clerks is £300 a year, of the magistrates' clerks £230, and of the Constabulary clerks £280, and I understand that the latter are not satisfied with their salaries.

418. Mr. Blackwood.—And have the Constabulary £280?—Yes, I understand that the maximum of the junior clerks is £280. Our salaries are also inadequate as compared with the salaries of the London Metropolitan Police Force, which is also an analogous establishment.

419. The senior clerks in the Constabulary rise to £450, and the rest to £280?—Yes.

420. Do you consider your position a superior one to that of a senior clerk in the Constabulary?—Oh, yes. I occupy a consolidated position.

421. Would you compare your position with that of the chief clerk in the Constabulary office?—Well, my office is supposed to include the offices of receiver, secretary, and supervisor of carriages. The salaries paid to those three officers originally amounted in the whole to £1,000 a year.

422. You have only occupied your office for two years?—Yes.

423. What were you before?—I was chief clerk in the secretary's department. At that time we had three clerks. There were three clerks of the first class, and I was the chief clerk of the first class.

D

October 22.
Francis Hinds, esq.

For many years, I may say, I had acted as working secretary to the department. Our former secretary was a barrister.

424. Lord Monck.—When were these alterations made that you speak of?—The alterations took place, I think, in 1860. The 22nd and 23rd Victoria, chapter 52, provided for these alterations. That Act provided that in the event of the retirement, or decease, of one of the Commissioners, an Assistant Commissioner should be appointed, the assistant to have £600 a year, and the salary of the Chief Commissioner to be £1,000 a year. Originally there were two Commissioners at £800 a year each.

425. Mr. Blackwood.—The salaries of the clerks, including yourself, are not fixed by the Act?—My salary is fixed by the Act at a sum not exceeding £300 a year.

426. Lord Monck.—Have you full employment for the whole of these clerks who are in the office?—Well, as a rule, we have, sometimes we have employment for more than our staff. We are obliged, under pressure, to get in one or two intelligent constables.

427. When you get constables in do you pay them extra?—No, they are not paid extra.

428. But they are taken off duty?—Yes.

429. You consider you could not work the office with a smaller staff than you have?—We could not work the office with a smaller staff. Very often I have myself to perform duties of a very mechanical nature indeed in times of pressure.

430. Mr. O'Reilly.—You say there is employment, and sometimes more for these clerks?—Yes.

431. Is there full employment for these clerks?—Of course, sometimes there is not, but we might have in one day occupation for double the number of clerks. Our staff is down to the lowest minimum.

432. I see that the registrar of carriages has two clerks?—Yes.

433. Is there permanent work an every day of the year for those two men?—No; I would not say every day in the year, but on some occasions, two or three times a year, there is work for more than two clerks.

434. But what I want to know is, could that office work with a registrar and one clerk, with the assistance of a couple of intelligent officers to do additional work occasionally? Would it work with a registrar of carriages and one clerk all the year round, and assistance as occasion required?—It would; there is no reason why it should not.

435. Lord Monck.—And on the other hand, supposing the establishment of the police proper was not increased, would not the Commissioners object to you constantly calling away men from the performance of their duties outside?—No doubt they would.

436. Mr. Blackwood.—Have you to obtain the Commissioner's authority for calling in assistance from the force?—Certainly. We make it a rule to call for as little police assistance as possible in our department.

We often remain after hours, and I repeatedly bring home work myself to facilitate business. There is a good deal of hurry and confusion in the daytime, answering questions and meeting the public, and it is only at night that one can concentrate his ideas for the preparation of important minutes.

437. With regard to the cost of dwellings, could you tell us what sort of houses the clerks usually occupy?—I am not exactly in a position to say. Speaking for myself, I know I pay very high rent, because I live in the country with other members of my family with land attached to the house.

438. Lord Monck.—You mentioned you had some recommendation to lay before the Commissioners?—Colonel Lake has requested me to state, that he considers a maximum salary of £250 a year for the junior clerks would not be unreasonable, and that the senior clerks should have a maximum salary of £370. The clerks would consider this sum not unreasonable, nor very large either. Colonel Lake thinks he could not recommend higher rates, in order to preserve the proper gradation of the several ranks.

439. Mr. Blackwood.—That would involve an increase of the minimum rates of the salary of the senior clerks?—Yes; the senior clerks would begin at £270, instead of £210, advancing by £10 a year up to £370; the accountant would begin at £400.

440. And the same for the junior clerk?—Yes; and in consideration of the long service of many of the clerks, Colonel Lake would be disposed to recommend an increase of £35 a year to those whose service exceeds twenty-one years.

441. Who is there that has served twenty-one years?—Well, the finance clerk has served that period, and the registrar of carriages, and the two senior clerks of the junior class. That would be four clerks. There are three junior clerks of the second class who have not served twenty-one years.

442. Does he make any recommendation about your salary?—He authorizes me to say he thinks my salary should be increased to the maximum, having regard to the fact that I hold a consolidated office—an office held by three gentlemen whose united salaries were £1,000 a year.

443. I suppose that was considered when the consolidation took place?—Well, I presume it was; but it was fixed at that amount then in consideration of two of the officers—Captain Williams and Mr. Ardagh—receiving pensions amounting to £500 a year. The other £500 was given to the accountant.

444. He recommends that you should at once receive the maximum of £500?—Yes, of £300.

445. With no prospect beyond that?—No; Colonel Lake would be disposed to recommend a higher rate, only that the Act of Parliament stops the way, and also indirectly affects the salaries of the clerks. The salary is fixed by Act of Parliament.

Doctor Thomas Nedley.

Dr. Thomas Nedley examined.

446. Lord Monck.—You hold the position of surgeon to the Metropolitan Police?—Medical officer.

447. Have you made inquiries into the relative pay and cost of living of the police in Dublin and the different cities in England?—Yes, I have received information from London, Liverpool, Manchester, Birmingham, Glasgow, and Edinburgh, and I hand in a tabular form the result of my inquiries. (See Appendix V.)

448. Mr. O'Reilly.—Is the regulated increase of pay more rapid in any of these forces than in Dublin, or in other words is the constable who begins at the lowest rank increased in pay by the regulations more rapidly in these forces than in Ireland?—In most of them as a matter of fact, having served a year he gets to a higher class and proceeds forward in each year.

449. Would you mention some of the forces in which that is the case?—In every force, except ours, that is the case; details and figures appear in the

Table. In Liverpool, for instance, the lowest rank has twenty-two shillings a week, after six months' service the constable's pay is raised to twenty-three shillings, after two years to twenty-four shillings, after three years twenty-five shillings, after six years twenty-six shillings, after nine years twenty-seven shillings; whilst the detectives there get from twenty-eight to thirty-four shillings a week. In all services, except that of Dublin, boots are allowed and officers' uniforms.

450. Mr. Blackwood.—Is there any allowance in other forces for the repair of clothes?—Not for the repair of clothes, but for boots only. In all of these towns the officers are allowed money for their uniform, but that is not so in Dublin.

451. Lord Monck.—You have explained how a man gets to a higher rate of pay, tell us now if the promotion is more rapid—I mean for the whole force—can one individual get to the top of the tree at the ex-

October 23.

Doctor Thomas
Nedley.

pense of others in most of the forces you have mentioned?—The Chief of the Police frequently advances a constable over the heads of other persons, in consequence of his superior merit, independent of the length of time he has served; and the pay of all constables is increased at a comparatively early period of service.

452. Mr. O'REILLY.—Do you include in that table, or could you add to it, in the different instances, the allowances to the other police, which may be considered substantial additions to pay, such as boots?—Yes.

453. Have you ascertained whether they possess special advantages with regard to lodging? I speak not of absolute money or lodging allowance, but special advantages, either in being supplied with lodgings gratis, or being supplied with special lodging at reduced cost, in any of the towns you have examined?—Yes, it exists in many of them.

454. Would you give instances of that, and explain them for us?—In London the Metropolitan Police have select houses in blocks, attached to the barracks, for married sergeants. These are very well built, and supplied with lavatories, sculleries, &c.; and for three rooms a sergeant pays 3s. 6d. a week. Sergeants who do not live in these, and who live out, pay 4s. 6d. for two rooms, and 6s. or 6s. 6d. for three, per week.

455. Lord MONCK—Were these houses built specially?—Yes.

456. By whom?—I should say by the Government or the metropolitan authorities. The one I saw and examined was at the back of Southwark Police Station.

457. Mr. BLACKWOOD.—Do you know whether these lodgings for married men entail any expense on the metropolitan funds, or whether the rents received pay the expense?—I am not sure with reference to London, but in Glasgow, where they do the same thing, the lodgings are cheaper, and the municipal authorities are completely recouped by the rents paid by the men. The rent is wonderfully cheap in Glasgow; for two rooms a man pays from 8s. 1d. to 2s. 3d. per month.

458. Mr. O'REILLY.—In Glasgow, are these lodgings specially built by the Municipal Council?—Yes, or adapted by the Municipal Council. The rents charged are sufficient to recoup the Board for the cost of the tenements, and the expense of their up-keep. It is a fact that in the city of London they have blocks of lodging houses for the men, cheaper than they could obtain them otherwise, but they do not recoup the city. In Birmingham lodgings are very cheap. There are a number of small houses built there—houses with two apartments, which is a great convenience, instead of tenements. The general cost for two rooms there is 3s. 6d. a week; for four rooms 4s. 6d. These are very good. I saw a very good house with two rooms and closet for 2s. 6d., but they were not occupied by members of the force; but you can get a two-roomed house for 1s. 8d. a week up a courtway, and these one-and-eightpenny houses are quite as good as the houses occupied by many of our married sergeants. But a more respectable class of house could be got in Birmingham by men who choose to do so. They can get a four roomed house and let a portion of it to the single men of the force.

459. Mr. BLACKWOOD.—Have you any evidence to show that if the married men were provided with houses of that kind it would have a beneficial effect on the health of the force?—I think it would. I am sure it would. That is, if accommodation were provided for them in blocks. There are in Dublin two or three houses for people—specially built for working people. Those people who occupy them certainly live more comfortably and enjoy better health than they would in the ordinary tenement house in low streets, at a cost of 2s. 6d. a week for two rooms. They have water-closets, bath-rooms, facility for washing clothes, and many advantages of that kind, and the rent pays the promoters.

460. And if the men were lodging in these blocks a good deal of labour would be saved, which is now devoted to the inspection of the men's lodgings?—

Certainly. They would likewise be more in hand, in case they were suddenly required, and it would be better for discipline also. The Chief Constable of Glasgow, writing to me about these houses, says—"It enables me to lay my hands more rapidly on them in the event of any disturbance or any necessity arising." In a large city like Dublin they ought to be provided with lodgings in different parts of the town. There are in many districts of Dublin houses that might be very rapidly converted into fitting houses for lodging a number of our men. There are large houses, for instance, in Eccles-street, and in Buckingham-street, and in Cumberland-street that might be got for this purpose for £50 a year.

461. Lord MONCK.—Colonel Lake informed us that all the unmarried men are compelled to mess together, as far as dinner is concerned, and that that is served to them at a fixed rate?—Yes.

462. Have you ascertained that that system prevails in London?—Yes, it prevails in various other towns.

463. Colonel Lake tells us that the cost comes to fix 4d. a week in Dublin?—Yes, and in the London Metropolitan Force, the cost of the dinner per week is something over 5s. 3d. from that to 3s. 6d.

464. That is the same as that for which they pay 6s. 6d. here?—Yes; it is a good dinner, and I think a better one than they get here, because, generally speaking, there is more variety. Our constables mess only at dinner. In consequence of their low rate of pay they cannot afford to buy a good breakfast, and the result is that they eat voraciously at dinner, sometimes to the extent of two pounds of meat being consumed by one man, but of course that is an exception. There is more meat therefore consumed at the dinners of the Dublin Metropolitan Police than in any other police barrack in the United Kingdom. In all the other barracks, with the exception of Glasgow, they are allowed three quarters of a pound of cooked meat. In Glasgow they are allowed half a pound of cooked meat, but the men always have meat for breakfast or eggs, consequently they do not require so much meat at dinner; and, as a matter of fact, in one of those towns, which I will mention presently, although there is only three quarters of a pound of meat allowed to each man, there is so much unconsumed that it is sold by auction as cold meat, and purchased by the men for their breakfast.

465. Lord MONCK.—That is the remains of dinner?—Yes

466. Where is that?—I think it is either in Manchester or Birmingham, although there is only three quarters of a pound of meat allowed to each man; that habit of taking so much meat at a meal acts on the men injuriously; many of them become dyspeptic—they are frequently placed on the sick list in consequence.

467. Mr. BLACKWOOD.—You say that the men are unable, from insufficiency of pay, to provide themselves with a good meal for breakfast. That may be the case with the married men, but is it the case with the single men too, who mess in barracks?—It is as a matter of fact; when I tell them to get a good breakfast they tell me over and over again they cannot afford it.

468. Lord MONCK.—When you come to take 6s. 6d. and 2s. 3d. for barrack stoppages out of their pay, they have not much left?—No; and, besides, everyone of our men is obliged to have a civilian's dress as well as a uniform, and that is costly.

469. Every man?—Yes, and they turn out uncommonly well at times.

470. I thought that was confined to the detective department?—No, it is not; I am aware that the men are desirous to be well dressed, and they do dress very well indeed on Sundays, or whenever they appear in plain clothes.

471. You told us the cost in the Metropolitan Police, as you have just detailed; give us any other particulars?—I alluded to the cost of living in barrack in Liverpool, Manchester, and other places; in each barrack the domestic comforts of the men are very

much attended to; they have baths, with hot water laid on at all times—in some places on each corridor; they have water-closets in every barrack, which is not the case in Dublin. They have a band in Birmingham and Liverpool.

472. Mr. BLACKWOOD.—Have the London Metropolitan Police any other advantages?—They have billiard-rooms and smoking-rooms, reading room, libraries, and glee classes.

473. Lord MONCK.—Are all those provided for them?—Yes. In Birmingham the men in barrack pay 7s. a week for dinner, lodging, and servants, and their breakfast costs 4s. a week, but there is not any mess except at dinner: in Glasgow and Edinburgh the men are not pensioned.

474. Not pensioned?—No; and if they are unable to work from sickness or other causes, they get no pay whatever.

475. You have told us what the police pay in London for house accommodation?—Yes.

476. Could you tell us what is the rent of two or three rooms in any other towns, apart from anything supplied to the police?—Yes; in Manchester, I am informed by the Chief Constable, Captain Palin—"Our sergeants and constables pay about 5s. a week for their house, which generally contains four rooms; many of the married constables have one or two constables to lodge with them, which reduces the rent."

477. Mr. BLACKWOOD.—I presume the Board of Works provide the fuel and light for the officers and barracks?—Yes.

478. And do the married men get any allowance for these?—No, not in Dublin, but they do in some other towns.

479. Did you enter into any comparison of the health statistics of your force as compared with that of any other force?—Yes; there are more men on the sick list in our force than in any other force in the United Kingdom.

480. Lord MONCK.—More men in proportion?—Yes, there is a larger percentage; if the man got more pay it would enable us to take off the shilling a day; that is the shilling that is stopped whilst the man is sick; in the city of London, I may mention, a man is sent off to hospital if he is only sick for a day.

481. Mr. BLACKWOOD.—They do not like to go to an hospital, I suppose?—They like it there, because they are well treated; there are great comforts for the men in London, and first-class treatment.

482. Lord MONCK.—Where is the hospital situated?—It is in the heart of London.

483. Mr. BLACKWOOD.—Have you any observation to offer with regard to your own remuneration?—Well, I think in proportion with the work that is done, our payment is small, compared with London.

484. You are allowed to practise besides?—Oh, yes; they are allowed to practise in every one of those places.

485. Mr. O'REILLY.—What is your salary?—My salary is £240 a year, and for that I have to attend every day, except Sunday, at the Castle, to examine recruits, and to sit on a board of pension, or to examine men as to their fitness for further service.

486. Mr. BLACKWOOD.—How many hours a day do these duties occupy you?—I could scarcely make an average; the extent of our district is very great.

487. Mr. O'REILLY.—You have not only, I take it, to attend at the Castle, but to attend each sick policeman?—Yes, I have; every sick man that is too ill to come to the Castle. When the cases are very bad we send them to the hospital; we have not to treat them there, but we have, of course, to look after them.

488. Mr. BLACKWOOD.—Who performs your duty in your absence?—The apothecary to the force, Dr. Long, who is called the assistant medical officer, who gets £50 a year.*

489. Would you say that your duties are as arduous as those of the surgeon of the Irish Constabulary?—

I think my duties are more arduous; my district extends from Dalkey—where there is a barrack, that I should say is about nine miles from the General Post Office—to Rossborough, that is the furthest end of the Phœnix Park—four miles; that is thirteen miles in one direction; from Crumlin, where there is a barrack—Crumlin, I should say, is three and a half or four miles from the Post Office—to Glasnevin, which is two miles from the Post Office, is six miles. That is a much larger district than exists in any force except London.

490. Are you allowed forage for your horse?—No.

491. Do you charge travelling expenses?—No.

492. Did you compare your salary with that of any other medical officer of the police force in England?—I did; the police force that most resembles ours is the London Metropolitan Police Force. The chief medical officer there has one hundred district officers under him, and those are the medical men who treat the sick members of the force. The duties of the chief medical officer are to attend twice a week in Scotland-yard, examine the recruits, and to report on the cases that are on the sick list for more than twenty-eight days. A police constable may request the attendance of the chief surgeon, but the case is generally attended by the district surgeon.

493. Is the chief surgeon allowed to practise also?—He is allowed also to do so; they do that everywhere, except in Edinburgh; but the medical officer there has other duties to attend to; he is the Officer of Health.

494. Mr. O'REILLY.—He is not prohibited from attending to other practice?—He is not actually prohibited from doing so; he is a professor, and has a class.

495. That is a sort of practice, of course?—Certainly. The Glasgow medical man gets £400 a year, and seven surgeons assist him, who receive £185 a year—amounting in all to £585 for a force much smaller than ours, and whose duty extends over less than one-fourth of our area.

496. Mr. BLACKWOOD.—Have you ever made any representation as to your salary?—Never.

497. How long have you filled your present post?—Since 1865.

498. Was the rate of pay your predecessor received the same?—The same; but since I joined there has been a good deal more severe duty, in consequence of the riots connected with Fenianism, and the general spirit of discontent that prevailed amongst numbers of the working people in Dublin and its vicinity, and the increase of injuries in consequence of their attacks on the police. There is really a great deal of responsibility connected with those cases, in consequence of severe injuries inflicted on the head, and the dangerous symptoms resulting therefrom; we have to watch them very closely. We have to see whether they are fit for duty—whether they are malingering or not. There is a great desire to get out while they are young on full pay, which they get if the injuries are received in the discharge of duty.

499. Are the duties of apothecary satisfactorily performed?—Perfectly.

500. Is he sufficiently remunerated in your opinion by the allowance that is granted to him?—Certainly not.

501. Mr. O'REILLY.—What does he do?—He has to come every day to the Castle; he has to compound the medicine, which is supplied to him—he does not supply it himself—he compounds the medicine, and to attend to cases in my absence; he has on several occasions done my duty in my absence.

502. Mr. BLACKWOOD.—Is it necessary for a gentleman in his position to compound the medicine?—Well, he does it; that was originally the duty which he undertook—formerly in Dublin there were two medical officers of equal position in the force.

503. But would not a chemist's assistant perform that duty?—If you had a chemist's assistant to do it, it would be necessary to have the assistant physician also.

* See C. Appendix IV.

504. Has the present apothecary made any representations as to his inadequacy of pay?—He has frequently to the Commissioners.

505. Does he perform the duty himself, or does he do it by means of an employé?—He performs it partly himself, and partly by means of his assistants—his assistants never come down to the Castle; he comes and gives the medicine to the men according as I order it, and we both sit together, the medicine is supplied by the Government.

506. And I take it that you consider that if the person holding the appointment of apothecary was not competent to render you assistance in the discharge of your medical duties, that you would be unable to discharge them wholly yourself?—Certainly; you can easily understand that with such an area as ours I could not do so. I might at any moment be sent to the Kill-o'-the Grange, seven miles away, and while I was going out there there might be a demand for my services on the opposite side of the Phoenix Park.

507. In fact, then, Dr. Long is the assistant medical officer of the force?—We do call him that from courtesy, in the profession, and from his position; strictly speaking, he was appointed apothecary—that is his official rank. He is apothecary to the Dublin Metropolitan Police. In all other forces in the empire there is a greater number of medical men in proportion to the force.

508. Lord Monck.—Do you think it would be a better arrangement, looking at the extent of your district, instead of having an apothecary in Dublin, to have what appears to be the case in London, one in every district?—Our barracks are too small, the suburban districts of London, as you know, are all crowded as cities—ours are country places, and in London there are a great many men in the different station-houses. With us there are some of those outlying stations which have very few men in them.

509. Looking at Kingstown or Dalkey, for instance, do you think it would not be better to have the men under the supervision of a properly qualified local medical practitioner, than to have an apothecary?—No; I do not think it would; I would get to Kingstown in a quarter of an hour, and in twenty minutes to Dalkey, if I received a telegram. A medical man living in town is more accessible than one living in the country, because his tours of duty, in doing his ordinary business, are not extensive.

510. Mr. Blackwood.—What do you consider would be fair remuneration to the apothecary for the duties he performs?—I think his pay of £50 a year is not enough, considering the duties he has to discharge; I think the raising of it to £75 a year would be very fair.

511. Is he entitled to a pension on the £50 a year?—Oh! I think he is; he has not sufficient pay; it is very seldom that he has to visit a patient. I think I have a great deal more duty to discharge than Dr. Holmes of the London Metropolitan Police; he has £600 a year, and has only to attend in Scotland-yard twice a week; I have to attend every day in the Castle; he has one hundred assistants to treat all the cases; I treat all the cases myself, except those that are so ill as to require to be sent to hospital. The total medical expenses of the London Metropolitan District, last year, amounted to £6,581 13s. 11d., and in Dublin to less than £350.

512. Mr. O'Reilly.—You have given us instances

of the salaries paid to medical men in similar positions to your own, with regard to the duties they discharge in connexion with the police force. Can you give us any particular instance of the salaries paid to medical men for anything like similar duties, for other public bodies in England as compared with Ireland?—I am under the impression myself that medical men are paid by local authorities more highly in Ireland than in England.

513. Mr. Blackwood.—Do you know whether the resident medical officers in the prison department—in Mountjoy and Spike Island, for instance—are allowed to practise?—Not in Mountjoy, but I don't know as regards Spike Island. However, that is since the appointment of the present medical officer at Mountjoy. Before that they did practise.

514. Lord Monck.—There is just one question I would like to ask you with reference to another matter. From your experience of the force, and looking at it in a sanitary point of view, do you think that the men are overworked, or, do you think the number of the force sufficient?—I do not think we have enough of men to do the work of the Dublin Metropolitan Police efficiently.

515. With due regard to health?—With due regard to health.

516. Mr. Blackwood.—I suppose they are not overworked often; the same man is not told off for night duty as well as day duty—he does not go on night duty after having come off day duty?—Latterly, in consequence of the deficiency in the number of men, they have frequently had to do duty for a longer period of time than is allotted in the regulations.

517. No extra pay is allowed for that?—No extra pay is allowed; men very frequently come to me, complaining of excess of duty as the cause of illness.

518. Lord Monck.—Looking at the matter from a sanitary point of view, do you think the time allotted by the regulations is as much as ought to be required of them?—Certainly, I think all the police in all the cities I allude to, have too much to do; a policeman, generally, who has been twenty years in the police, looks from ten to twenty years older than he really is, police duty, in fact, in my opinion, ages men more than any other duty performed by any classes that I am acquainted with. I was asked what advance of salary would be fitting to give to the apothecary, but you did not ask me what I considered my own should be.

519. Mr. Blackwood.—Well, we shall be glad to hear you on that point now!—I think that £300 a year is the least that the Government ought to give me for doing the duties which they call on me to discharge, having no allowance for rent, for forage, and having such an extensive district to attend to.

520. Suppose that you were allowed forage in addition to your present pay of £240, would that satisfy you?—I would be glad to get it.

521. You would be satisfied?—No, I did not say I would be satisfied. I would be glad to get it; I would be glad to get forage for two horses.

522. The surgeon of the constabulary receives £37 a year for forage?—£37 a year, and he has a house, coals, gas, and servants.

523. If you were allowed £37 a year for a horse, would that meet your views?—If I got the forage of two horses, I would be content. I require two for my duty.

---

524. Lord Monck.—You were asked to come back again, because I have had two or three suggestions upon which we should like to have your opinion. Dr. Nedley was here just now, and has made a very lengthened statement, and furnished us with returns of the condition of the police in London, Glasgow, Manchester, and other places, and he mentioned that, in one of them, when a man enters the force, if he be

a well-conducted constable, he advances from one grade to another in his rank, from year to year, as a matter of course. The consequence of this is that the number of constables in the highest grade is very large, and the number in the lowest grade is very small. The direct reverse is the case in the Dublin police; now, what is your opinion as to what would be the effect of this system on the efficiency of the Dublin police

October 21.
——
Colonel Henry
Aswell Lake,
c.b.

force, what would be the effect on the force by each of the two systems: it is of course a question of money?—There is no doubt that it is a question of money, and would increase the expenditure immensely. The first-class constables get 19s. a week, and there are only a certain number of them. Then, as vacancies occur, either from promotion, resignation, or dismissal, their places are filled up from the next grades.

525. Perhaps I failed to convey the meaning I wished, when I put the question. Supposing we are prepared to recommend an increase of pay to all the grades, would you leave the gradation as it is at present; would you make a small increase in the pay of the lower rate, and leave the man to go on to the higher, or would you give him an addition to his pay each year?—I think it would be better to leave the principle as it is at present. I think it would be better and more satisfactory than what is proposed.

526. Dr. Nedley also stated that in some instances, in other police forces, the system of promotion from one class to another is managed much more by selection than it is in your force. What do you think of the introduction of that system of increase by the principle of selection?—Is it into the higher grades?

527. Lord Monck.—Into the higher from the lower grades?—No; I would leave the lower grades as they are up to the grade of acting sergeant; but I would beg leave to suggest that the following should be the proportion in each rate of constable in lieu of the present:—first rate, 375; second, 168; third, 333; fourth, 50; total, 826, exclusive of the detective division.

528. With regard to the grades, I think you told us yesterday that up to the rank of acting sergeants the promotion went principally by seniority?—Up to the grade of first-rate constable promotion is by seniority, and then there is an examination after that.

529. When you hold a competitive examination—as I understood your answer yesterday, your plan is, that after a certain number of men are examined an approved list is made out, and no further examination is made until that approved list is exhausted?—Yes.

530. We had a very intelligent constable here yesterday, who thought he could have got on the list if he were admitted to the examination, and his idea was that there should be an examination periodically for the number of vacancies that existed; that you should keep no approved list, but should open the examination again according as vacancies occurred. What is your opinion about that? Do you think his suggestion worth accepting, or would you rather leave it as it is?—Certainly; and I really think his suggestion ridiculous, for, in the first place, I should then have to hold an examination for every vacancy, whereas I hold an examination of a certain number of constables, and those whom I select I place on the approved list, and then according as a vacancy occurs I put a man in that place.

531. Is your list limited to a certain number?—No; that is altogether according to what I may consider desirable.

532. Could you tell me as a matter of fact how many you have on the approved list now, in round numbers?—The present is a very unusual case. The last examination I had from first-rate constables for acting sergeants, I put a certain number on the list, and then those who were not on the list sent in a memorial stating that however low down they were on the list they would be satisfied, but that they wished to be on the list. And then, owing to the promotions having been more rapid than usual, and that the men on the approved list had disappeared very fast, I made out a supplementary list of men who had really passed a very good examination, and whose characters were very good. Therefore, the list at the present moment is larger than usual; but I would say that on an average I would put twenty on the list.

533. What relation does that number—suppose that we assume 20 as the number—what relation does that number bear to the probable vacancies that occur within a year—what proportion did you absorb within the last two years?—That depends on certain cir-

cumstances—how many men go before the medical board.

534. Do you promote twenty men every year?—There were more than twenty men promoted last year.

535. Mr. BLACKWOOD.—Do you think it would not be a good plan to hold these examinations every year, instead of every five years, so as to give some chance of promotion to those who had entered the service lately? The complaint appears to be that when once the list is made out for the five-yearly period, a man, no matter what his capabilities may be, has no chance of getting promotion?—I see what you mean. It is a mistake to call them five-yearly. For instance, an examination took place in March, 1864; another in March, 1865; again in 1867, and the last in 1871. On ordinary occasions, when the list is not too large, as in the last examination, I think it is quite sufficient, and it is the best way to hold an examination, when the list is exhausted, and not to make it too large. Then I don't think the younger constables will have cause of complaint, for they will come up in time.

536. But all depends on the size of the list?—Of course it does; and I think I explained to you that this list was bigger than ever before. There was a great pressure put upon me by men who had acquitted themselves well, who were of undoubtedly good character, and good constables. I broke from my general rule and put a larger number on the list; out of this list we have many men getting into trouble, and they are removed from the approved list, and many a man is invalided, and many a man leaves the force.

537. Lord MONCK.—I did not quite gather from you whether the men were placed on the list in the order of merit as they passed from the examination, or in the order of seniority in the force?—I will explain that. I give a certain number of marks for the various subjects of examination—reading, dictation, spelling, and so on. And then I give a certain number of marks for efficiency in the service and, to a certain extent, for seniority—that is for the number of years they have been in the service. I add all these up together, and then the men are placed in order according to the totals they got—according to the whole numbers.

538. They are placed according to their merit in the examination, their seniority and efficiency being elements in the result of the examination?—Yes. It very often happens that one man comes out at the head of all as to reading, writing, spelling, &c.; but I know almost every man in the force, and when I come to inquire of the superintendent, I am informed confidentially, that although so clever in these other respects, he is not an efficient constable.

539. Mr. BLACKWOOD.—We were asking Dr. Nedley if he did not think a system whereby married men could be accommodated with lodgings erected at the public expense, putting a certain rent on them sufficient to repay the cost in time, would not be an arrangement satisfactory to the force, and tending to efficiency, health, and good discipline; and he said he thought it would be, and instanced the cases of several cities where they have that in operation. Have you ever considered the point?—Oh, yes; I have, very often. I think nothing would tend more to the respectability of the force, if I may use the term, than this arrangement you propose now, for this reason, that I am afraid that owing to straitened circumstances many of them live in houses not only unhealthy, but altogether unsuitable to their position.

540. Have you ever thought how it could be carried out—whether such buildings should be erected by the Corporation of Dublin, or by the Government?—I am very much of opinion that the Corporation of Dublin would have nothing to do with it, owing to their having no degree of control over the police force—it being a Government force; but I think that if it was undertaken by the Government that it would eventually pay for the outlay.

541. In your report to the Irish Government, on the 26th of March this year, you stated at the close, that should Government be pleased to take steps for im-

proving the condition of the Dublin Metropolitan Police, there is every reason to believe that the citizens of Dublin were prepared to take their part in assisting in a work that would be so conducive to public interests?—Yes.

542. You mean by that an increased police rate?—Yes.

543. The police rate is now 8d. in the £1?—Yes, 8d. in the £1.

544. What steps are necessary to increase the rate—have they it in their own power?—The Government have not power to increase the rate, I think. A new Act of Parliament would be required for the purpose.

545. What grounds have you for entertaining this opinion contained in the report?—Only from the opinions I have heard expressed by my subordinate officers, who mix a good deal with the people, and who tell me that they say there is no rate so willingly paid as the police rate, and that the citizens of Dublin, who are more or less favourable to the police, would not object to a small increase.

546. An increase of 1d. in the £1?—Yes; an increase of 1d. or 2d. in the £1. I have a memorandum here to show how much it would yield.

547. Mr. O'REILLY.—Are you aware that the maximum rate that can be imposed in London by Act of Parliament is 9d.?—No; I am not aware.

548. I suppose that if the Dublin people were to know they pay nearly as much as the London people, they will think they pay enough?—I have here the information about the rate, if you like to hear it. The police tax, assessed at 8d. in the £1, was fixed by the Act of Parliament, 1st Victoria, cap. 25, and was passed in 1837. If it was increased by 1d., making it 9d., it would produce an additional income of £3,000 a year.

549. I want to ask you one question on that. Is that on the old valuation of the district, or has the re-valuation of the district been carried out yet—is it on the old valuation or on the re-valuation which would make a considerable difference?—The assessment of the police rate under 1st Vic., cap. 25, was made on Sherrard's valuation, and on a special valuation made by the Police Commissioners of the suburban districts under the Act.

550. Mr. O'REILLY.—We have gone over with your accountant and secretary the question of filling up some of the clerkships from the police force. I should like to ask your opinion of the following proposals. . That the accountant or secretary, the finance clerk, and one clerk in the Secretary's office, should be drawn from the class of clerks in the ordinary acceptance of the term?—That is to say, outside the force?

551. Yes; and that the registrar of carriages and four other clerks who appear to be required, should be drawn from the police force itself—the registrar of carriages to have something like the salary of a superintendent, and the four clerks also, with the salaries of sergeants. What do you say to this scheme?—I approve of it with this exception—that I think the registrar of carriages ought to be taken from outside the force.

552. Mr. BLACKWOOD.—May I ask your reason?—Yes. It is a very important situation, and he has to be mixed up a good deal with the public, and I think this furthermore, that a person outside the force is more calculated to conduct the duty, and in a more satisfactory way, than if you employed a man from the force.

553. But supposing that the registrar of carriages were a superintendent who was promoted to the post, he then would be outside the force; he would be no longer a superintendent of the force, he would be registrar of carriages?

554. Lord MONCK.—We don't mean that this man, when he came into his new position should remain in the force any longer?—You mean that he should be removed?

555. Mr. O'REILLY.—The proposal is simply to promote a superintendent of the first class?—May I ask you one question first: would you make the office permanent, or what would it be?

556. Mr. O'REILLY.—The registrar of carriages certainly to be permanent, and the others an open question?—I think that the registrar of carriages under these circumstances might be taken from the force.

557. Mr. BLACKWOOD.—You see, some very large increases of pay are applied for, which will amount to a very considerable sum on the whole, and of course it is our duty to see whether we cannot suggest some alterations which will bring about a reduction, however small. Now, we conceive that if men of the rank of sergeants and acting inspectors were employed as clerks, they would be receiving considerably less sums than the clerks now in the offices, but giving them an increase also at the same time?—Yes, I understand; it would be considered a boon to the force. It would create a very good feeling in the force.

558. Lord MONCK.—When we asked Dr. Nedley, as to the remuneration of his apothecary, he stated that both he and the apothecary were underpaid, and said he thought that an addition of £60 a year to his own salary, making it £300, and £25 to that of the apothecary, making it £75 would be a fair increase. What is your opinion of that? If I were asked what would be a fair remuneration for the apothecary I would say that £100 was not too much for him, and, besides, he has to do a good deal of duty for Dr. Nedley when he is away. And I think £300 a year very fair for Dr. Nedley, in his position as physician.

559. Mr. BLACKWOOD.—The accountant was authorized by you to state that his salary might fairly be raised to the maximum at once?—Yes; I did.

560. That is to say that he should be raised from his present rate at one jump from £370 to £500 a year?—Yes.

561. That is his maximum?—Yes. He has been more than thirty years in the service, and he is an energetic and efficient man.

562. But he has been only two or three years in the place he now holds, and he has been receiving the annual income of £370 for only that time?—I only give you my opinion about it.

563. But if he receives the £500 a year now it would be nearly as reasonable to suppose that he should have received it two years ago. Is there any reason for saying he should receive it now more than two years ago?—No; but when the gentleman who occupied his position went out he drew very nearly the maximum, and Mr. Hinds, the present accountant, when he came in thought he ought to get the same—that he was entitled to it, and so did the Commissioners.

564. Don't you think it would tend to simplify matters if the accountant were called chief clerk or secretary, there seems to be some confusion now between the accountant and finance clerk?—I should prefer his designation being changed to secretary, because he is, bond fide, secretary.

565. Lord MONCK.—But he is bond fide accountant, for he is responsible for the accounts?—Yes.

566. Mr. BLACKWOOD.—Chief clerk, I think, would be the best?—Very well; but secretary, for various reasons, would be a better title. I think you asked me one or two questions yesterday that I can answer now. You asked me what was the rate of messing formerly and what it is now. The system of messing was established at different periods in the several divisions. It is now universal throughout the force, as regards unmarried men. In the C division, messing first commenced in 1864. I find that in 1864, the rate was 3s. 10d. per man per week, for seven days; it is now 6s. for six days, and the meat is said to be of an inferior quality. In the D division, the rate was in 1864, 4s. 3d. per man per week, for six days; and it is now 5s. 6d. In the E division, I can only trace back as far as 1867, when the rate was 4s., and it is now 5s. 6d. In the B division, the rate was in 1867, the date of messing being first established in this division, 4s. 6d. per man per week, and its present rate is 5s. 10d. With the exception of the C division

October 23.

Colonel Henry
Atwell Lake,
C.B.

in 1866, these rates only include six days, Friday's dinner being a separate charge. In consequence of the increased price of meat, and of potatoes having risen from 3s. 10d. per cwt. in 1868 to 7s. 6d. in 1872, the men, on an average, consume only 6½ lbs. of meat per week, instead of 7½, which was the usual allowance per man in 1867.

567. Lord Monck.—You also told us that you would be able to give us the relative population of the metropolitan district now, and at the time the police force was first established.—When the force was first established, in 1838, its strength was 911 ; the population within the district, then about twenty-one square miles in area, was something like 240,000 , its present authorised strength is 1,088; the population now numbers 337,589 within a district of thirty and a quarter square miles.

568. Mr. O'Reilly.—I see that the accountant has £40 a year for keeping a horse. What is the peculiar reason why he should keep a horse?—Because the police barracks are vested in him, and he is supposed to be the officer who regulates the barracks, and to see that they are kept in the terms of the leases. He ought to visit the barracks periodically, and I suppose that the £40 horse allowance is a conveyance allowance.

569. How many barracks does he visit, and how often does he visit them?—I am not prepared to say how often he visits them, but the barracks are very much scattered—there may be about twenty of them.

570. Mr. Blackwood.—Does he keep a horse?—I believe he does. There is one circumstance that the force are very anxious that I should bring to your notice, and which is a great hardship If a man suddenly dies in the service—and there have been several cases, from apoplexy and other complaints —before the medical officer could certify that they were past recovery, and the necessary papers made out for their receiving the usual gratuity; in such cases the family of the deceased have no claim whatever for the gratuity, and there have been three or four cases within the past five or six years, where an inspector and an acting inspector have fallen dead suddenly while in the discharge of their duty, and their wives and children received nothing whatever from the Government. There is a small sum of money vested in my name in the bank, called the Widows' Fund, to which the men have long since ceased to subscribe, and it now amounts to a very small sum indeed—something under £300. Out of this fund I generally give the widow a certain sum if her husband dies in the service. In consequence of the family of the deceased man getting no assistance in any other way, the force at large is obliged to subscribe—as has been very often

the case—to keep the family out of the workhouse. What I wish to request is, that in cases of this kind the widow or the family of the deceased may receive the gratuity which he would have received had he lived long enough to have had his papers made out.

571. Lord Monck.—Is the constable who becomes suddenly ill and incapable of duty entitled to a gratuity no matter in what state of health he may be?—In the case of an officer or constable being reported by the medical officer as either being in articulo mortis, or not expected to live, his papers are made out for the gratuity to which he is entitled, and application is made to Government for permission to give him this amount.

572. Lord Monck.—And is that application as a rule, granted or refused?—Always.

573. Mr. Blackwood.—That is where the gratuity is given after death?—Yes, in cases where the application is made prior to death.

574. Lord Monck.—It is a question of degree then, and the cases I should say are very rare? I know they are rare indeed. But there was the case of an inspector, who had served between twenty and thirty years, and was absolutely at work at the time; he went to the mantel-piece in the office to get a drink of water, or a piece of bread, and he fell down dead. He left two children but no wife. There is one other subject. When I was speaking about the mounted police, I forgot to mention that the officer in charge of them—the inspector—also has applied for an increase of his pay on the same grounds as the men—that he had to purchase more than if he was in the foot police.

575. Lord Monck.—In fact that the same principle which applies to one, should apply to all?—Yes. You were asking what were the actual stoppages from the men. There is 8d. per week for barrack-rent, 6d. per week for fuel, and other things are stopped from the men, not before they get their pay, but as they are getting it, by the barrack-sergeant.

576. Mr. O'Reilly.—But still they are supplied?—Yes. I think you asked about the detective police—how much their uniforms cost. They only get one suit of blue uniform in six or seven years, because they only have to wear it when they are attending as witnesses in the court-house. The average cost of the uniform and appointments of a constable is £6, and therefore there is so much saved, and they have to find their own plain clothes.

577. Lord Monck.—The force has never been materially increased since its original foundation?—No.

Adjourned.

November 6.

John A.
Browne, esq.

NOVEMBER 6, 1872.*

John Augustus Browne, esq., examined.

578. Lord Monck.—What position do you hold in the service?—Registrar of carriages under the Commissioners of Metropolitan Police.

579. What is your present rate of salary?—£390.

580. Your minimum is £210, and your maximum £330?—Yes.

581. How long have you held the office?—Since 1858, when I was appointed registrar.

582. Your present scale of salary was fixed in 1868?—Yes. I was appointed in 1858 at a fixed salary of £150 ; in 1859 a scale was introduced for the first time.

583. What was that scale?—£160, by £10 a year, to £260.

584. Until what period did that scale continue in operation?—In '68 the maximum was changed from £260 to £300 ; in '71 the maximum was increased to £320, and the minimum to £210.

585. What are the duties of your office?—The licensing of all car proprietors, tramway cars, job

proprietors, cabriolet proprietors, and the drivers and conductors thereof, under the Dublin Carriage Acts of 1853, 4 and 5. We also receive a yearly duty of 10s. from each hotel proprietor and publican within the police district—they number between 1,000 and 1,100.

586. What are the particular acts which that involves on your part?—There is a return (hands in return). We first have to take an application from the party, such as that (hands in document).

587. The first duty you have to discharge is to receive applications for licences?—Yes, and we are obliged to instruct the parties in filling up the forms of application ; we then send the parties to the carriage inspector's office, with a view to having their vehicles inspected.

588. Is the carriage inspector a branch of the metropolitan police force?—He is a sergeant in the police, specially appointed for carriage duty, under the superintendence of the detective force, and has a staff of con-

---

* The intermediate days were taken up by the enquiry into the Royal Irish Constabulary.

stables under him, to see that the by-laws are carried out, and that the rules are complied with. When we get back this report (refers to document), we then have to write each licence in duplicate, such as that (refers to document), and send it to the proper officer for signature.

589. Mr. BLACKWOOD.—That work is filling up printed forms?—Yes.

590. Lord MONCK.—Then what have you to do?—Then the party applying comes back at an appointed time, and we issue the licence and got his receipt on the back of the duplicate, which we retain.

591. Do you receive any money?—Yes.

592. There are fees payable on all these licences?—Yes; about £6,000 a year.

593. You receive these?—Yes.

594. What do you do with these fees when you receive them?—I lodge them every week in the bank to the credit of our accountant.

595. Mr. BLACKWOOD.—Are you bound to lodge them every week?—Every week, according to our arrangements.

596. But is there any regulation to that effect?—Yes; that is the practice of the office, and has been always.

597. You are responsible for these moneys until lodged in bank?—Yes, until I furnish the bank docket to the accountant.

598. Lord MONCK.—Do you give any security?—Yes.

599. What?—£400.

600. Mr. BLACKWOOD.—Have you any payments to make?—No payments.

601. Lord MONCK.—Tell us what other duties you have got to perform?—Perhaps if I trace the history of a licence you would understand it better. We have a register, in which we have to write the date of grant, the name or names, residence, where it is a company, the name of the public officer, and the style or title of the company. We also have to enter the licence in an alphabetical book (we keep a street alphabet of these licences), with the numbers, the name, and residence. Then these licences are subject afterwards to be transferred from one party to another (hands in the form of transfer, involving the writing of the number, the names, and residences of both parties, and their signatures; the same process has to be gone through as with the original licence.

602. And all that has to be done in your office?—Yes. The licence is subject to a change of residence; we are obliged to take an application from the proprietor—his name, the number and description of his vehicle, from what place to what place, and his signature; and that has to be posted in both the books, the register, and the alphabetical. The licence is also subject to be surrendered, involving the writing of the name, the number, the residence, and the date, and posting in both books. If the plate we issue be lost, the owner has to apply for a new one, and before taking his application he is obliged to make a declaration as to the loss. When the declaration is supplied we issue a pass for a week, writing the name, residence, description, and for what period the pass is in force, in duplicate.

603. That is to enable the traffic to be carried out while the new plate is being prepared?—Yes, and to give an opportunity to have the old plate recovered. I may state that up to a recent period these persons who might chance to lose their plates, owing to the system in the office, were obliged to remain for three days idle, and it was at my suggestion the Commissioners adopted the plan of giving passes, so as to enable poor men to work their vehicles. At the end of the week the owner comes back with his licence, and we receive his application for a new plate. We have to post the new number on the back of the licence, and on the back of the duplicate, and we have to enter that in both books. All the particulars of the old number has to be re-written after the new number, which is a different one. We then have to send a return to the carriage inspector of any change, involving the writing

of the name, residence, description, and number, so that he may see that the old number, if recovered, is not used. The licence is also subject to be suspended for a time for bad repair, or misconduct on the part of the proprietor.

604. By whom is the suspension to be decided?—A report from the carriage inspector is forwarded to the Commissioners, and they order the suspension or revocation. We then fill the necessary form, containing the description of licence, date of grant, name, residence, nature of offence, period of suspension, and date of Commissioners' signature. We have also to fill up a notice in duplicate, with same particulars, calling on the owner to deliver up his licence and plate. We keep a separate record of all suspensions, and the parties concerned have to come twice to the office. In January and July a printed notice, with the name and residence written in it, has to be served on each car proprietor, who must pay an annual duty on his licence, in order to keep it in force. At the periods fixed for the purpose, certificates, signed by me, are issued on payment of the duty. In each certificate the name, amount, number of licence, date, and signature have to be written on block and counterpart, and the payments have to be posted in the alphabets from which the particulars are taken. The particulars of each day's receipts are entered on a pay sheet, and forwarded to the accountant with a daily abstract. The amount of labour and responsibility involved can be estimated when I say that there are over 6,000 registered persons, and that each of those persons, on the lowest average, comes to the office five times in the year, thus causing more than 30,000 regular transactions every year. There are three periods of extreme and two of moderate pressure in the year, and it has always been found necessary to have extra aid to enable us to get through the necessary work on those occasions, when 200 or 300 persons have to be attended to in the day. Of course you will understand that in the keeping of the books of a registry of that class we are obliged to be very particular as to correctness. Our office is the only public office under the Commissioners, and the public generally come there for information respecting the registry of all car proprietors with whom they may have disputes. We have to refer to the books, and in most cases to write the name and address for those persons, in order that they may go to the police courts to get summonses out; and they expect us, as it is a police office and a public one, to give them the information they require. We have also to file a pay sheet of each transaction that occurs every day, and lodge it, with the daily abstract of all the moneys paid on the different classes of vehicles. In February, 1869, the Commissioners thought it advantageous to transfer the drivers' registry office to my charge. The order says:—"The drivers' registry and carriage registry shall be under the registrar of carriages, Mr. Browne, who shall be responsible for both these branches." I was than called on to report as to the state of the drivers' office, and to suggest any improvements that would be advantageous for the department. In the absence of the secretary, the Commissioners authorized me to sign the carriage and drivers' licences, and for a considerable time I discharged that duty. Finding that I had no compensation for that responsibility—for it is a responsible thing to have to do, because I would be liable to an action if things were wrong—I took the opportunity, when taking my vacation, to ask the secretary to resume the duty, which he did.

605. And has the secretary since that time signed all licences?—Yes.

606. Is the same process, which you describe, as regards carriage licences, gone through with reference to applications for drivers' licences?—Substantially, the difference being that a driver has to come once or twice oftener to the office, and all offences of which he may be convicted, and the penalties imposed on him by the magistrate, have to be posted into the drivers' register. I think that is all as regards the carriage drivers' business. As regards the publicans I spoke of, we

E

November 6.

John A.
Browne, esq.

first have to send them a notice to come in and pay. After they have renewed their licence in the Custom House, they have to pay 10s. to the police as a special tax. When they come in we have to instruct them to fill the name, the residence, the parish, and the date they pay the excise, and the date of signing. In many cases we are obliged to fill the form for them ourselves, in order to facilitate them. A return, each morning, of the number of certificates issued the previous day is furnished to the superintendents of the different divisions. These returns embrace the name, the residence, and number of certificate—the date in two places. The certificates we issue are in duplicate, and contain the name, residence, parish, date, and signature, and the payments have to be posted in the publicans' register.

607. So much with regard to your duties. Now, with reference to your salary, have you any complaint to make on the score of salary?—I have been always complaining of its inadequacy.

608. On what is your complaint grounded?—As a class complaint. I think my salary as a first-class clerk ought to be at least equal to that of the first class clerk in the constabulary, which is to an extent a similar establishment.

609. What office did you hold before you were appointed to your present position?—I was appointed in 1849 as supernumerary clerk in the rent office—it was the first appointment I may say I ever had—at a salary of a guinea a week.

610. What was your next rise?—In 1851. I was placed on the staff at £70 a year; in 1853 my salary was increased to £80 a year by promotion; in 1854 the salary was increased to £100 a year.

611. Mr. Blackwood.—In 1853 you got £80?—Yes. In 1854 it was increased to £100, in consequence of reductions in the staff and changes in the department. I might say I was in the carriage rent office, it was a distinct office from the carriage registry office. At that time the two offices were amalgamated. The principal clerk of the rent office retired on pension, and I was the only clerk of that office who was transferred to the carriage registry office, and who knew the business of the place. The registrar of carriages, the late Mr. Eola, did not understand the business of the rent office, and all the first-class duties devolved on me, although a junior, from 1854, when I was transferred to his office, up to 1858, when I was appointed to his place.

612. Did you continue the same from 1854 to 1858?—At the close of 1854 I got £115 a year.

613. Would you tell us what was the next increase in your salary?—In 1858 my salary was raised to £160; that was the fixed scale of the registrar. In 1859 there was a new scale, from £160 to £260; the changes of the office in 1864 involved the doing away with several of the gentlemen, and there was a superior of the carriage department attached, at £250 a year, which was the fixed scale, and the next office to which I could have expected to have been appointed. That office was abolished in 1859, to which I might reasonably have expected to be appointed. I had to wait ten years under the new scale before my salary could come up to that amount;

I took the liberty of sending in a statement to your secretary, explaining my individual grievance. I need not, I presume, repeat anything that is therein referred to?

614. With regard to the general question, have you any complaint to make as to the salary, because it seems to have been revised very often and very lately?—It was so laid in the beginning, and the room for an increase so large, that all that has been done for me leaves me in the position of a second-class clerk in the constabulary, and other similar offices even in Ireland, although I have been discharging, since 1854, first-class duties, and bearing the responsibility which was formerly divided between the registrar, the office collector, or chief clerk, and three out-door collectors. I may state that it has always been understood by the officers of this department that their prospects have been most injuriously affected by the very unusual act of a former supervisor, a Mr. James Fagan, who retired in 1850 or '51, and who refused to accept the full amount of the salary of his office, on the ground that he had either one or two pensions from other departments in which he had served. This course naturally kept down the salaries of those under him.

615. What office in the constabulary would you compare yours to?—A first-class clerk's; I submit that the duties which I have to discharge in the public service deserve a higher scale of pay than those who are sitting in a private office whose duties are not more important; I may also state that I am bound to find security, and the majority of the clerks in the constabulary have not to do so. In a public officer great care is required—in fact, any error of mine might involve the Commissioners in an action; the reason that I desire to compare the constabulary office with ours is that both are police establishments.

616. Mr. O'Reilly.—Is there any other ground on which you would like to base your claim for an increase of salary?—Yes, the great difficulty of supporting my wife and six children; the children are young, and I have to keep up a respectable appearance, but it is impossible for me to do so on my present salary. I have been compelled to get evening employment to enable me to keep out of debt, in consequence of the small salary I receive and the large amount I have to pay for every class of provisions.

617. Has this pressure on you increased of late years?—Largely; everything that has to be provided for a household is at least a half more than it was a few years ago.

618. Have you compared your salary with the salary of any of the officials in the ranks of the metropolitan police with which you are acquainted?—The Commissioners recommended in 1860 that our salaries should be assimilated with that of the police court clerks.

619. I did not ask you that; what I have asked you is, have you compared your salary with the salary of the officials in the ranks of the metropolitan police? Of the force?—I never did; we are quite a distinct branch of the department; the only comparison that can be gone into is with the criminal branch, the magistrates' clerks.

Christopher
Duignan, esq.

Christopher Duignan, esq., examined.

620. Lord Monck.—What position do you hold in the public service?—I am the finance clerk in the accountant's office of the Police Commissioners' department.

621. How long have you held that office?—For nearly twenty years.

622. Your present scale of salary is £310, rising to £320 a year?—Yes.

623. Mr. O'Reilly.—And you are now at your maximum?—Yes, I have arrived at it this year. I entered the service as junior clerk in the police tax office on 22nd May, 1842.

624. Lord Monck.—What was your salary then?—

Fourteen shillings a week for three months, and then I had a guinea a week for five years.

625. What year was that?—In 1842.

626. How long did you remain on the salary that you had in 1842?—Three years, and then I got £60.

627. When did you get the next increase?—In 1851, £90, and in the year 1853 I was transferred from the police tax office to the Commissioners' office as second clerk in the receiver's office, which is now the accountant's office.

628. What was your salary then?—£120 a year.

629. What was your next increase?—After three

years, when the Chief Clerk retired, I was appointed to his place, and got £150 a year.

630. That was the fixed scale?—It was.

631. That was in 1855?—In 1856.

632. How long did you remain on that salary?—Until the late Mr. Seaton from the Treasury improved the scale.

633. What was the date of that?—1859.

634. What did you get then?—An increase at the rate of £10 a year.

635. You were put on a rising scale then?—Yes.

636. What was the minimum?—£160.

637. What was the maximum?—£360 a year.

638. That continued until when?—Until 1861.

639. What occurred then as regards your salary?—I got an increase to £210.

640. That is £210, and rising to £330?—Yes.

641. Mr. BLACKWOOD.—By that?—By £10 a year.

642. Lord MONCK.—And you are now at your maximum?—I am.

643. Were you not given some steps one year?—I do not mean the annual sum fixed some short time since?—Yes, on the representation of Captain Williams.

644. What was the increase?—It was increased by £30.

645. That is, you got a jump of three years?—Yes.

646. What year was that, do you recollect?—It was the year 1861.

647. Mr. O'REILLY.—Who was Captain Williams?—He was the last receiver.

648. Mr. BLACKWOOD.—On what grounds was the increase of £30 granted to you in 1861?—Long service, and the nature of the duties which I had to discharge—the responsibility attached to the duties which I had to discharge.

649. A similar increase was granted to Mr. Hinds?—Yes; I was then virtually and substantially doing all the receiver's duty; I discharged both his duty, and the duty of pay clerk, &c.; at present I pay all the pensioners.

650. Lord MONCK.—Would you describe to us what your duties are?—My duties are to check and keep all the principal accounts connected with the Metropolitan Police establishment; I have to check all the claims, and to furnish monthly the accounts to the Comptroller and Auditor-General in London.

651. Mr. BLACKWOOD.—Do you sign that account?—I initial it, and Mr. Hinds signs it.

652. Would it not be more correct to say that Mr. Hinds furnishes the account monthly to the Comptroller and Auditor-General?—Yes, strictly speaking.

653. Lord MONCK.—Mr. Hinds, I take it, is responsible for them?—He is responsible; I send it to him ready furnished, and he examines each item, and signs it.

654. He is the responsible officer?—He is the responsible officer, by law.

655. Have you any other duties to discharge except those which you have mentioned?—The principal responsibility I have is the payment of our pensioners, monthly and quarterly, which amounts to about £26,000 a year.

656. How are those persons paid?—Those who receive their pensions monthly are paid in cash, and those who are paid quarterly by cheques, bank bills, &c.

657. Who signs them?—Mr. Hinds signs the cheques, and they are counter-signed by the Commissioners, and then I pay them to the parties.

658. How do you obtain the cash to pay those men?—By an order given on the Paymaster-General, and his cheque is cashed in the Bank of Ireland.

659. Who signs those orders?—Mr. Hinds signs them, and one of the Commissioners counter-signs them.

660. Have you to give security to pay out this money?—I have to give £800 security—two securities in a joint bond.

661. To whom do you give this security?—To the Crown.

662. I believe there are other duties that you have to perform?—Another branch in the store; I have to superintend the checking of our stores which are considerable, and include the uniform, clothing, bedding, &c., and the unclaimed and forfeited property,

and to see that those things are properly disposed of annually, and to check the return of the money received for forfeited property and old stores sold by auction.

663. Do you act as the storekeeper?—I am a check over the storekeeper.

664. Then you have a storekeeper?—Yes; he ranks as an inspector of police, and a tailor who ranks as a constable.

665. Mr. BLACKWOOD.—Who is responsible for the store accounts—who signs them?—The storekeeper signs all those documents.

666. I mean the store accounts?—The store accounts and the cash account, that is the forfeited money; that is signed by the storekeeper, and I check and sign it, and the balance that is unclaimed is lodged in the Bank of Ireland to the credit of the forfeited moneys account, quarterly.

667. But there are store-books, and matters of that kind?—They are supposed to be under the immediate charge of the accountant; he is the responsible officer for those things, and the storekeeper is his deputy, who is acting for him.

668. Just as you are his deputy in another department?—Yes.

669. Lord MONCK.—Is there any other part of your duty that you would like to bring before the Commissioners?—I think I have enumerated the principal duties I have to perform. I prepare the annual estimates for the Treasury.

670. In the absence of the accountant on leave or from sickness, who performs his duties?—I have been always called upon to act for him in his absence.

671. When you perform his duties, do you perform them all—do you sign cheques?—I do not sign cheques, unless he got some very lengthened leave.

672. I am assuming that he is away for a month or six weeks; I sign all those orders I spoke of on the Paymaster-General, but I would not sign cheques without first having received authority from the Treasury; I have never in that capacity for two receivers—for Captain Williams and his predecessor.

673. When you are acting in that capacity you check the accounts just as the accountant would do?—Just in the same way.

674. When you are performing the duty of the accountant, who performs the duty of checking your own account?—Myself.

675. Do you check your own accounts?—I do; but they are re-checked by a clerk to the Commissioners down stairs. There is no account passed without being checked by one of the Commissioners' clerks; they are first checked by me, and I see that the claims are properly made, and to guard against any risk at all, the clerk to the Commissioners examines them and certifies them, and they are then authorised to be paid by the Commissioners.

676. Mr. BLACKWOOD.—Do your duties as finance clerk, as a general rule, occupy the whole of your time?—The duties require constant daily attendance and close application.

677. What are your hours of attendance?—I generally arrive in the office at eleven o'clock in the morning, and I remain until four, five, or six o'clock, as the business may require; I have attended in the office during those hours since the new system of accounts came into operation—since 1868—and I did so purposely for my own convenience, to save the annoyance of discovering errors; I keep all the balances square, and they are never questioned by the audit office.

678. Mr. O'REILLY.—Is there any rule as to leave of absence?—The general rule is to give the clerks a month's leave once a year, but I never take any leave.

679. Lord MONCK.—Have you any complaint to make?—Have you anything which you would wish to bring before the Commissioners?—Nothing except what they are all complaining about—the salary is too low after such a long service.

680. Mr. O'REILLY.—On what would you base your claim for an increase of salary?—Long service and the responsible nature of the duties of the office, and also the enormous high prices of the principal necessaries of life.

E 2

November 6.

Francis Molton, esq.

Francis Molten, esq., examined.

681. Lord MONCK.—What position do you hold in the Civil Service?—I am senior clerk in the second class of the Metropolitan Police department.*

682. How long have you been in the service?—Nearly thirty-seven years, since the formation of the establishment.

683. What is your present salary?—£200 a year.

684. What position did you originally fill when you entered the service?—A clerk in the Metropolitan Police Commissioners' Office.

685. When was that?—In the year 1836, when the Metropolitan Police force was first established.

686. What was your salary then?—It commenced, I think, on £50 a year, but I was very young at the time.

687. Then what was your next rise?—There was an increment of £5, at a maximum of £75.

688. From what date?—From the date of my appointment.

689. When did you get the next increase?—The next increase was when Sir T. Redington was Under-Secretary.

690. Give us the date?—1847.

691. What was the rate then fixed?—£110 a year.

692. Fixed salary?—Yes.

693. An increase from £75 to £110?—Yes.

694. What was the next increase in your salary?—The next was an increase of £110 to £140, by an increment of £5.

695. What was the date of that?—1850.

696. What was your next increase?—Then there was a further application to the Treasury, and they raised the £140 to £190 by an increment of £10, and they increased it to £200 afterwards.

697. When was that?—In 1867; it was then fixed at £190, but they raised it to £200 afterwards.

698. Which department are you in?—In the secretary's branch of the Commissioners of Police.

699. You are in the accountant's branch?—In the secretary's branch of the Commissioners' office.

700. What are the duties you have to perform?—Writing letters, minutes to Government reports, and correspondence for the department.

701. I presume that you get a minute from the accountant and you expand it?—No; from the Commissioners.

702. Mr. BLACKWOOD.—Do your duties occupy the whole of your time?—Altogether.

703. What are your hours?—From ten to four.

704. Have you ever to stay beyond that time?—Frequently; during times of political excitement, such

as the Fenian, there was a considerable amount of work to be done, and that continued for years; and then there was also the arms licensing.

705. Lord MONCK.—We have got the duties and scale of salary of your department before us, and now we would be very glad to hear you if there is any other observation that you would like to make?—There is one observation I would like to make, and that is with reference to the suppression of a first-class clerkship, a junior class clerkship might be suppressed, but not this first-class; I should have succeeded to that office by seniority if it had not been suppressed.

706. By whom was the first-class clerkship suppressed?—Through a Commissioner who has since retired—not the present Commissioner.

707. Mr. BLACKWOOD.—I presume it was done by the Treasury?—By the Treasury; I have a letter of the Treasury, and you will see that they were reluctant to suppress the first-class clerkship.

708. Mr. O'REILLY.—Would you be entitled as a matter of right to the succession of that first-class clerkship?—Certainly, by the usages of the Civil Service; there was no one before me.

709. Do you attend here as the representative of your department to seek for an increase of the salaries of the clerks in your office?—Yes.

710. What do you wish to say on their behalf?—On their behalf, I have to say that they are underpaid, compared with the second class clerks of the constabulary and other offices having analogous duties to perform.

711. Lord MONCK.—Is there anything else that you wish to bring under our notice?—Nothing, except that I find is hard to live on the salary I have of £200 a year; £300 a year is not more now than £100 a year was some years ago.

712. Do you find a pressure on you from the lowness of your salary, and that it has perceptibly increased as compared with a former period?—Very much so.

713. Within what period would you say that has been the case?—Perceptibly, I would say, within the last five or six years.

714. That period you speak of is since your salary was fixed?—Yes, since my salary was fixed; but there is a greater grievance which I have to complain of, and that is the suppression of the office I alluded to. This is felt by all the second-class clerks, as an injustice, inasmuch as it narrowed the field of promotion in the department.

Francis Hinds, esq.

Francis Hinds, esq., recalled.

715. Mr. BLACKWOOD.—We asked you the other day how far a superior class of policeman would be qualified to discharge the duties of the office of registrar of carriages, and your answer in effect was that there was no objection to the employment of such a person, except that he must be in every respect qualified as to character, responsibility, and experience?—Just so. He must have some experience of accounts, and receive money, and account for that money properly.

716. It appears to us that those duties, with the exception of the receipt of money, are of a mechanical kind—they consist in the filling up of forms?—Altogether of a mechanical nature.

717. Then the greatest responsibility that rests on him is attached to the receipt of money?—Yes.

718. Is it absolutely necessary that he should receive the money—I mean, would it not be possible for him, instead of receiving the money, holding and paying it to the accountant at the end of the month, to hand to the person applying for a licence a document which he (the person) could then take to you, and pay the money over directly to you?—The only objection to

that is that he would have a great crowd of carmen coming to the office in the Castle every day, which, I am afraid, would inconvenience the Commissioners very much. The registrar of carriages has a distinct office in College-street, adjoining the police station, and the object of that is to prevent the overcrowding of our office with carmen.

719. Lord MONCK.—Would it not be possible, by an arrangement with the bank, for the registrar of cars to give to each of those men an order authorizing the bank to receive the amount of his licence, or whatever the payment might be, and put it to your credit ultimately, so that no money should pass through the hands of the registrar?—I have no doubt such an arrangement would be practicable. If you give me time to consider it, I will let you know what could be done.—(See Appendix "VI.")

720. Mr. BLACKWOOD.—Assuming that some arrangement could be made to obviate the receipt of cash by the registrar of carriages, there is no objection to the employment of a police officer of experience and respectability in that position?—None whatever.

* See B, Appendix IV.

William Williams, esq., examined.

721. Lord Monck.—What position do you hold in the police office?—Chief clerk in the southern division of the police courts.

722. How long have you held that position?—Since 1862. I was first appointed in 1837, and attained to my present position in 1862.

723. Your salary now is £250 a year, rising by annual increments to £350?—Yes.

724. What is the salary you now actually receive?—£350 a year.

725. You attained to that position when?—In 1862.

726. What position had you held previously?—I was always in the public service from my youth up.

727. What office did you first hold in the public service?—Junior clerk at Arran-quay police office; I may state that at that time there were four divisions in Dublin.

728. When were you appointed?—By Lord Mulgrave on the 16th of September, 1837.

729. What was the salary you then received?—The salary at that time was £75 to the junior, and £130 a year to the senior clerks.

730. £75?—Yes.

731. That was in 1837—how long did you remain on that salary?—For about two years.

732. Until 1839?—Until 1840.

733. What was the next increase in your salary?—£130 a year.

734. Was that as a junior or senior clerk?—The chief clerk above me retired, and I got his place.

735. You had a fixed salary of £130 a year?—Yes.

736. How long did you remain on that salary?—Until 1862, when I obtained my present situation; in the interim Mr. Seaton increased the salary at Kingstown court by £100 a year additional. I was then in that court.

737. Then you got £230 a year in 1859?—Quite so.

738. In 1862 you got your present appointment?—Yes, first going up £10, and afterwards £15 a year.

739. Mr. O'Reilly.—You say that you were appointed a chief clerk in 1840?—Yes.

740. How many divisions were there in Dublin at that time?—Four.

741. Were they subsequently consolidated?—They were, one by one—first the office that I was in, and I was then transferred to the head office; subsequently College-street office was abolished, and the business sent to the head office, and now the northern and southern divisions have been established since we got into the new courts.

742. Now, there are only two courts in the city?—Yes.

743. Lord Monck.—Will you be good enough to tell us what are your duties?—A thorough knowledge of the whole criminal law, in the first place; to be able to make out a warrant for any criminal, to draw out informations, and lay them before a magistrate, and also to instruct the five gentlemen who are under me.

744. You have got five gentlemen under you?—I have.

745. How many second class clerks are there in each office?—There are five in mine, and one in Kingstown, which is a sub-office connected with the southern division.

746. You have five junior clerks in each office, and one in Kingstown?—Yes.

747. What are your hours of attendance?—From ten to four o'clock each day, or longer if necessary; sometimes we have excise cases, when we must stay for a longer period; I have been there as late as six o'clock occasionally, but the usual hours of attendance are from ten to four o'clock.

748. Have you any complaint to make with regard to your position generally?—Yes; that where a clerk holding the same position as I do in London commences I end; he commences there with a salary of £350 and goes up to £500 a year.

749. I have no doubt you are aware that there is a good deal of complaint all through the civil service as to the inadequacy of the present scale of salaries?—I don't know what the feeling is in any other department but my own.

750. Mr. O'Reilly.—Supposing a vacancy occurred in your office, how would it be filled up?—It should be filled up by the next senior competent man in the service who is only to be found in the department.

751. In the second class?—Yes; there is much technical knowledge required for the office.

752. Then would you tell me how the vacancies in the second class clerks in your office are filled up?—There are only two classes in my office.

753. When there are vacancies amongst the second class clerks in your office how are they filled up?—By competitive examination.

754. Can you tell me how your office is classified for competitive examination?—It is classified.

755. What class is it in?—I do not know the classification at all; but I know that it has been frequently rejected by gentlemen who have passed the examination, and who have gone elsewhere.

756. Was the office at the time filled by competition?—At the time I mention?

757. Yes?—Very recently it occurred. A gentleman came in to ask the particulars of the office, and on learning them he would not take it, but went away to London or Edinburgh.

758. Do I understand you that there was an instance of a young man who, having succeeded at the competitive examination for the public service, on finding he was entitled to select a position in your office, on ascertaining the particulars of the service, declined to take it, but selected one in London or Edinburgh?—Yes. The young gentleman I allude to selected an office in Edinburgh.

759. Mr. Blackwood.—Has the vacancy in your office been since filled up?—It has.

760. By a gentleman who is a competent person?—I believe he will turn out a very competent person; but it is right to tell you that there has been an improved scale for the junior clerks. The salaries they had have been advanced from £70 to £90 a year.

761. Lord Monck.—Is there any other statement you would like to make?—I don't think I am paid commensurately with the duties that have devolved upon me since the amalgamation, nor do I think that the intermediate clerks between me and the gentlemen who enter at £90 a year have reason to be satisfied. They are here, and will state that more particularly.

762. Mr. Blackwood.—But still they accept their positions with a full understanding as to the rates of salary to which they may rise?—Yes; with the understanding and hope that they will be improved. It is only right to state that the clerks in the police courts have duties of a much superior nature, mentally, than those of clerks in other offices.

763. I suppose that the examination fixed for entrance into the police courts by the authorities is considered to be a fair test of the qualifications of the men?—I have no doubt it is. The duties devolve upon me to teach the recruit.

764. Lord Monck.—When did the consolidation of the offices take place?—In 1868.

765. Did that throw additional duties upon you?—It did.

766. Are your duties sufficient to occupy your whole time?—Quite so; that is, the general supervision of the whole office.

767. But not to overtax you?—I am sometimes overtaxed, but not as a rule; I am equal to a good amount of work. There are sometimes very serious cases in our courts that keep me till six or seven o'clock—taking excise cases, and so forth. I have as fair a share of work as any other servant.

768. Mr. Blackwood.—Then you base your application for increase of salary more upon the grounds of the duties you perform than upon the increased cost of living?—Upon both; for £100 a year when I first joined the service was worth £200 or £300 now.

November 9,
———
William
Williams, esq.

769. Mr. O'REILLY.—Would you base your claim for increase of salary upon the increased cost of living between the date at which it was fixed and the present time?—The cost of living has risen very considerably.

770. Would you base it on that?—I would. The only matter that I would wish to bring before you personally—and I do it as much in the interest of the clerks under me as for myself—is this—I was away from the office for nine months from the foundation

of the first Fenian persecutions, carrying them on with a late chief magistrate, Mr. Stronge. I merely mention the fact, not for any egotism, but in order to show the number of very responsible duties we are called upon to perform. After I had been with Mr. Stronge, he told me that I had the honour to be reported to Lord Kimberly for distinguished public conduct; but his Excellency replied there was no fund out of which I could be rewarded. I only mention that to show the character of the men with whom I am associated.

Edward S.
Dix, esq.

Edward Spencer Dix, esq., examined.

771. Lord MONCK.—What is your position?—I am one of the divisional justices of Dublin, and I was appointed in August, 1867. I have been five years a magistrate.

772. What was your salary when you were appointed?—Just as it is now, £800 a year.

773. Were you previously in the public service?—No; I was practising at the bar.

774. Do you know when the salary was fixed at £800 a year?—No; it was some years previously. Originally the divisional justices had much less. At first there were six police courts, with three magistrates in each—the Government only having the appointment of one. They were, an alderman, who was appointed by the old corporation, an ex-sheriff, and a barrister of seven years' standing, whom the Government appointed. Then in the time of William IV. that was changed, and the appointment of all was given to the Lord Lieutenant. He must appoint a person who is a practising barrister of seven years' standing. Then the Lord Lieutenant had the power of reducing the number, and that was done, the courts being reduced to three, viz.:—the College-street police court, the Capel-street police court, and the Head office. The magistrates had then only £600 a year. Afterwards the number of magistrates was reduced to five, who were to preside at two courts in Dublin, and also at Kingstown. When I was appointed in 1867, I was attached to what was known as the Head Office. That court was the most wretched ever seen, with the worst accommodation and ventilation—it was the Southern court. The Northern divisional magistrates held their court in a house in Capel-street, and this was a shade better than ours. Now the Government have built a court at the back of the Four Courts—one every way satisfactory—with everything we could ask for, in the way of ventilation and accommodation. When I was first appointed the informations were taken as they had been ever since the police courts existed in Dublin, in this way—the prisoner was brought forward, and the witness was examined by a magistrate, and the case was heard. As soon as he had made up his mind as to what was to be done with the case, the witnesses were ordered to go into the clerk's office and there their depositions were taken in writing by one of the clerks. Then they were brought back into court, and there the depositions so taken down by the clerk, were read over in the presence of the prisoner to the witness, and the latter signed them. But some of the judges objected to that mode of taking the informations, and the Law Advisers wrote their opinion that the proper way for having informations taken was to have them taken down by a clerk in the court, word by word from the witnesses, as was done at petty sessions. Our answer was, that to do so we should require a larger number of clerks, and after some time, they were given. These clerks had to pass a severe competitive examination, and we have now no complaint to make of want of staff. They are all thoroughly occupied, and I believe that we could not do with half a one less. On Mondays, in the Southern court, we have about 100 prisoners, and I believe they have nearly as many in the Northern court. It takes two clerks for court duty on Mondays. We are satisfied now with our staff. We don't want more clerks, and having due regard to the public service, we could not do with less than we have.

775. They don't complain of pay?—The clerks do, and the public do not complain of the way the work is done.

776. You have a sufficient number of clerks to perform the duty, but not too many?—Yes.

777. How many hours do you attend?—We are due to sit at ten o'clock, but the sheets are not arranged by the police clerks until about half-past ten, when we commence, and we are bound to sit till four. There are five magistrates for the three courts.

778. Mr. O'REILLY.—And the courts sit every day?—Three sit every day. One is at the Northern Court, one at the Southern, and one at Kingstown.

779. Have you any statements to make with regard to the rate of payment?—I speak for myself and the two Mr. O'Donnells, my colleagues. I had not an opportunity of consulting the other two. I think that the police magistrates of Dublin are inadequately paid, having regard to the salaries of the London police magistrates, and the statistics will show who has to do the largest amount of work.

780. Mr. BLACKWOOD.—When you were appointed were you satisfied with what you received?—Quite so—perfectly. I knew that all I was to get was £800 a year, and I gave up my practice at the bar for it. But the reason given for the London police magistrate getting so much more was, because it was so much more expensive to live in London than Dublin—

781. What have you to say on that point?—My own opinion is that I could live nearly as cheap in London, with the exception of house rent. I would say, with that exception, the London magistrate is in much the same position as to expense of living as we are in Dublin.

782. Lord MONCK.—On what is your notion of house rent in London based?—On general knowledge. A relation of mine recently rented a small house in Eaton-terrace, not half the size of my house in Mountjoy-square, and he paid a far higher rent than I do.

783. Mr. O'REILLY.—What rent do you pay?—£85 a year, and taxes about £30.

784. What accommodation have you?—Two parlours, two drawing-rooms, two bed-rooms on one floor and three on another, and other apartments. It is an ordinary-sized house in the square.

785. Mr. BLACKWOOD.—Would you consider that your house in Mountjoy-square, for which you pay £85 a year and taxes, is twice as large as a house in Eaton-terrace, in London?—I would think so. Except as to house rent I do not believe there is much difference between London and Dublin in the cost of living. I believe that the cost of food is much the same; but perhaps servants' wages are not so high in Dublin.

786. Lord MONCK.—You have spoken with reference to your own salaries, and with reference to the nature of the work, have you any remark to make with reference to clerks' salaries?—I have not gone into that.

787. Mr. BLACKWOOD.—Do you consider that the duties of the clerks in your office are satisfactorily performed?—Perfectly; we have got a very efficient staff of clerks. As to ourselves, I think that, having regard to the duties of our offices, and our position, and the far larger salaries of the London magistrates, our salaries are not adequate in proportion.

788. Mr. BLACKWOOD.—Do the members of the bar in Dublin obtain as much remuneration as members of the bar in London, as a general rule?—They do, only the amount of business is not so great. We have men who do a good deal, but nothing like the business of the leaders at the English bar.

789. But do the members of the bar in Dublin obtain as large remuneration as the members of the bar in London?—That depends upon the class of business they are doing.

790. But putting barristers in Dublin against the barristers in London, and striking an average, which of them receive the largest income?—I will not take it upon myself to answer, but there is a much larger amount of business in London than here.

791. And that makes a larger income?—Yes.

792. Therefore the conclusion is that the barristers in London are in receipt of a larger income than the barristers of Dublin?—I could not take it upon myself to say that. The men at the Irish bar may not have the business or receive so large an income as some of the barristers in London.

793. Mr. O'REILLY.—But taking the barrister in reasonably good practice, not first-rate practice, could you give us an idea of what his income would be?—That depends on whether he would have a silk gown and divers other matters.

794. Can you give us an idea of what a barrister in reasonable practice would make by his professional emoluments?—I cannot; but I knew one barrister who made £7,000 a year. I need not mention his name; he was a Queen's Counsel, and is dead. He did a great Rolls business, and it is many years since he practised. None of my acquaintances ever made more.

795. Lord MONCK.—There is just one other question I would like to ask : is there any want of a supply of barristers of seven years' standing to take your place?—No, indeed there is not.

796. Mr. O'REILLY.—And you could get them reasonably good?—Indeed you could.

Edward Davis Daly, examined.

797. Lord MONCK.—What position do you hold?—I am one of the second-class clerks in the Dublin Police Courts.

798. How long have you been in the service?—Eight years and six months.

799. Was the position of a second-class clerk in the Police Court the first office you held in the public service?—Yes.

800. You were appointed in what year?—In May, 1864, at the time I was appointed I was a third-class clerk (which class has been abolished); I have never been in any other service.

801. Your salary is on the scale with a minimum of £90 and a maximum of £330?—What is the salary you actually draw?—The salary I actually draw at present is £125 a year; the scale under which I was appointed was £70, rising by £6 to £190. The scale under which I am paid at present is as you have stated. The new scale was provisionally adopted by the Treasury in August, 1867, but I did not receive a penny of that until May, 1870, when I received the first increment of £10.

802. Mr. BLACKWOOD.—What was the reason of the delay?—If you will allow me, I will go shortly into the history of the case. [The witness referred to a correspondence with the Treasury, relative to the three years during which the second class clerks then holding office had not received the annual increment under the new scale, but he was informed by the Commissioners that they could not entertain the matter, it being retrospective in its character.]

803. Lord MONCK.—Do you think the present rates of salary are inadequate to command a supply of competent men to perform the duties of the office?—My belief is that they are not adequate.

804. Upon what is that belief founded?—It is founded first on the knowledge I have of the special aptitude that is required for the very difficult duties of our office, and I say, arguing from my own experience of young men, that you will not get persons properly qualified to perform those duties except they have gone to considerable expense in preparing themselves by education for the office, and the prospects of promotion here are not sufficient to satisfy those who have done so ; and the second reason is—and this has been my experience of late, that young men proposing to enter into the public service have come to our office and inquired as to the salaries, and have gone away and refused to enter the department.

805. Are there any vacancies in your office for second class clerks at present?—Not one.

806. Have there been any vacancies lately?—None from resignation of junior clerks.

807. Had any vacancies to be filled up from any cause?—Yes.

808. Within what period?—Within the last couple of years.

802. How many vacancies have occurred to your recollection?—There were two. It was with reference to those two that the persons of whom I spoke came to make inquiries.

810. Those vacancies have been filled up?—Yes.

811. Are you acquainted with the gentlemen appointed?—Yes.

812. Are they competent men?—That is a very difficult question for a junior clerk to answer. I do not wish to express an opinion.

813. Mr. BLACKWOOD.—We have already got the evidence of the chief clerk that they are really competent men?—I see no objection to what he says.

814. Mr. O'REILLY.—How did you obtain your appointment?—By nomination.

815. At that time, eight years ago, the scale of remuneration was sufficient to attract competent men to the service?—I had great difficulty in ascertaining what the scale of remuneration was, and when I entered the service I found it was different from what I had believed.

816. Now vacancies are filled up by open competition?—Yes.

817. Lord MONCK.—Assuming for a moment that we are not going into a comparison between the London and Dublin officers, have you any statement to make with regard to the inadequacy of pay founded upon other grounds?—If I may be allowed to go into a personal matter, I would say that after eight and a half years' service, £125 a year is not enough for any person who is expected to keep up the ordinary decencies of life, to live in a respectable locality and to clothe himself so as not to be unlike those with whom he mixes, especially if, as is the case with most young men, there are others depending upon him, and there are other responsibilities likely to grow up.

818. But when you entered the service did you not know that was to be your condition if you continued in it?—I was then young, and I really did not know very much about the scale of remuneration. I made several attempts to find out the scale of remuneration I was accepting. At the time I was not very well off, and had to take the best thing I could get, and I thought the chances of promotion would have been greater.

819. But that is not a reason for the Government varying the bargain?—Of course, if the Government chose to take that tone, and tell us you have made a bargain and must stick to it, we have very great difficulty in denying our share of the bargain ; but I am not aware that every employer outside the Government service would hold his employees to a bargain made at a time since which the condition of the service has changed.

820. In what respect has the condition of the service changed?—In the cost of living.

821. That is a perfectly good ground upon which to

November 6.

Edward Davis
Daly.

ask for an increase of pay; what have you to say on that point?—I only mention it. I leave the evidence with regard to the increased cost of living to other members of our service, being aware that they have given their special attention to the subject. There is one matter to which I would call your attention, and that is, that the duties we have actually to perform are more difficult and harassing than mere clerical duties—than mere copying of documents or writing correspondence. I wish also to leave on record my own view, as the result of my personal experience, that if my present situation was offered me, with the present scale of salary as it stands, and the present prospect of promotion, I should not accept it.

822. Would not you qualify that by saying "if you were beginning life;" because there is nothing to prevent you leaving it at present?—That is what I mean. If it was now offered me. The reason I do not leave is, that it is better for me, after eight and a half years' service, to stay on at a disadvantage than to commence in a new sphere. Another point we desire to bring to your attention is the superiority of the London scale of pay, and the greater number of senior appointments there. Here the older members of the present junior class do the duties of senior clerks, without increased pay. The chief duties of our department are greater than can be performed by the two chief clerks unaided.

William Miller

William Miller, esq., examined.

823. Lord MONCK.—What position do you hold?—I am one of the clerks in the Northern Police Court. I was senior clerk until about two years ago.

824. Mr. BLACKWOOD.—Are you chief clerk?—No; I am a finance clerk.

825. Lord MONCK.—What is your rate of pay?—£220

826. Mr. BLACKWOOD.—And your scale of pay—I do not mean the actual pay you receive?—When I was appointed my scale was from £70 to £130, and then from £130 to £330 by £10 a year.

827. And what have you come here to say?—The time that the junior class and my class were amalgamated the minimum salary of their scale was given an increase of £30 a year, that is, from £70 to £90, and the maximum was made £230, the same as that of my class, and I feel it a grievance that the clerks of my class were overlooked and amalgamated with the junior clerks.

828. That is a matter that relates to the past, not to the present?—The price of living is so much increased and there has been no additional remuneration in any way, although the business of late has also increased very much. I think, if I was allowed to suggest anything, it would be, that the promotion in the office is too slow. There are now only two out of thirteen clerks in the department who are chief clerks. That is the only promotion in the office, and my grievance mainly is, that there is no intermediate class, such as existed when I first joined, between the chief and the junior clerks; and the finance clerk is on the same footing, as to pay, as a junior clerk. I have twenty years' service now, and I think that the finance clerk should have a scale higher than those beneath him.

829. But is your complaint that the present rate of pay for your class is insufficient, in consequence of the increased cost of living?—Yes; I know that the cost of living is nearly doubled during the last ten years.

830. Do you consider that rent has increased?—I do.

831. Mr. O'REILLY.—What is your grievance as a class?—I have mentioned want of promotion, and our department is underpaid with reference to other departments in Ireland. We have very responsible work.

832. Mr. BLACKWOOD.—You say that your class is very much underpaid?—Yes.

833. Do you think there would be any difficulty in supplying a vacancy in that class?—In what way?

834. If a vacancy occurred, would there be any applications for the post by properly qualified gentlemen?—Yes.

835. Then you think there would not be any difficulty?—I am sure not.

836. Have there been any vacancies lately?—A few for the last two or three years.

837. How have they been filled up?—By Civil Service gentlemen.

838. Have they been filled up by gentlemen who can discharge the duties of the office? They come in there as clerks, but they have to be instructed.

839. Of course they have. That occurs in every office?—As to competency, I myself, if I wanted promotion to-morrow, must go to another man. I will not be asked am I competent. I would not like to say whether a man was competent or not. The head of my department is to say whether I am competent or not; for the first question is, "Have you got the chief of your department to recommend you as a competent man?"

840. You say that this class of clerks is underpaid; at the same time you state that vacancies are filled up by gentlemen who have passed a competitive examination for them. Does not that show that the remuneration is sufficient to attract gentlemen who, in the opinion of the Government, are qualified to perform the duties?—But a great number of them, when they come to the office to inquire after it, have refused to take the place, in consequence of the pay not being the same as what it is in other places in the country. I know several.

Adjourned.

November 7.

Joseph Wm.
O'Donnell, esq.

NOVEMBER 7, 1872.

Joseph William O'Donnell, examined.

841. Lord MONCK.—What position do you hold?—Chief of the police magistrates.

842. Is there any observation you would like to address to the Commissioners with regard to your own position?—The only observation I would address to you is the inadequacy of our salaries compared with the London magistrates, taking into account what we have to do, and the great increase in the price of all the necessaries of life for the last twelve or fourteen years. Admitting there may be some items of expenditure greater in London than in Dublin, and making every allowance in favour of the London magistrates, we think the disparity between their salaries and ours is most unreasonable and unjust. Their salaries compared with ours is as 12 to 8, and the chief 15 to 9. From what I know of my own knowledge, and have

heard and read on the subject, I believe the work is equal if not more here.

843. As a matter of fact is it not the case that legal officers and counsel are paid more highly in England than in Ireland?—They are paid higher than here, but not much.

844. The Lord Chancellor in England gets a much higher salary?—I don't think so; he gets £10,000 a year, and our Chancellor gets £8,000.

845. Mr. BLACKWOOD.—When you accepted your present office did you raise any objection to the inadequacy of the pay as compared with the pay of the London magistrates?—It never entered into my consideration at the time, and perhaps should not do so now if it were not for the great increase in the price of the necessaries of life.

846. You base your case mainly on that?—I base my case mainly on the increase of the cost of living. I came to Dublin in 1852, and I have kept an accurate account of my expenditure in each year, and I can safely say there is an increase of nearly two-fifths in the cost of living in Dublin, as compared with that time. In other words, that a pound will do now what twelve shillings did then, and no more.

847. Mr O'Reilly.—When were the present salaries of your office fixed?—In 1859. When I was first appointed there were seven magistrates at £600 a year. At the time of my appointment the Government intended to reduce the number and increase their salaries, and a bill was brought in in 1859 reducing the number to five, and increasing their salaries to £800. I was appointed chief magistrate when Lord Kimberley went out of office, and after a good deal of correspondence with the Treasury, I got an increase of £100 a year about eighteen months ago. When I was appointed at the close of 1855, there were seven magistrates at £600 a year, the gross amount of whose salaries was £4,200. Then there was the act in 1859 enabling the Lord Lieutenant to reduce the number of magistrates and the offices, and providing that where the magistrates did not exceed five, for an increase of salary; the gross amount of the latter, however, was not to exceed £4,200.

848. Mr. O'Reilly.—Then, as I understand the argument, that is put forward by you as to the change in the salaries which would be due to the increased cost of living, assuming they were rightly fixed at first, it would apply to the change in the cost of living from 1859 to the present date?—Most assuredly; £800 a year will not go as far now as £600 a year did in 1859.

849. Lord Monck.—As far as I can understand you, your case for an increase of pay is based mainly on the increased cost of living?—Yes.

850. And that, from your own expenditure, you can state that the cost of living has increased in Dublin fully two-fifths?—Very nearly, if not fully, two-fifths since 1859, because the great increase has taken place since 1859; you know the price of meat is double.

851. Mr. Blackwood.—Have you the chief control of the clerical work of the police courts, as performed by the clerks now in the establishment?—I have not; the chief control of the subordinate clerks belongs to the chief clerk of each court, and then he superintends the performance of the duties of his subordinates, and if there be anything going on that should not take place he refers it to me.

852. Then you are qualified to give an opinion as to whether the work is satisfactorily performed or the contrary?—I am; because no clerk could be admitted, after temporary probation, without my certificate. The course in our department is this—the clerk stands a competitive examination, and is passed; he is then sent to the office for six months probationary period and at the expiration of that time I must certify to the Civil Service Commissioners my approval or disapproval of his conduct and competency; but before doing so I make the most searching inquiry as to both. And as regards the superannuation of clerks, no clerk can get his superannuation unless I give a certificate

that the discharge of his duty has been satisfactory to my mind.

853. There have been vacancies within the last three years which have been filled up by competition?—Yes.

854. Is the work performed by the officers who have filled these vacancies, so far as you know, satisfactorily performed?—Perfectly.

855. Do you think that any of the duties of the establishment could be satisfactorily performed by subordinate officers of the force being detached for those duties—I mean an inspector or acting inspector?—Do you mean of the police?

856. Yes—Decidedly not.

857. Are there any of the duties of the second-class clerks which consist merely of copying, and could, therefore, be performed by writers?—Not strictly so; perhaps the nearest approach is the filling of summonses, and even in these cases a certain discretion must be exercised. There has been a long correspondence between myself and the Treasury in reference to the appointment of writing clerks, and I satisfied the Treasury of the utter unfitness of that class of persons for office in the police courts. The result was that the two appointments you allude to were made. In fact, all the subordinate clerks are preparing themselves, by constant court practice, for the chief clerkships. Apropos to that, though I don't see how it could be done—I cannot see my way to it; but, so far as I can judge, I think the junior clerks are perfectly satisfied with their salaries, as long as they remain such; but they would look forward, if it could be done, to have some graduated promotion beyond what at present exists, only two of the thirteen clerks now in the department being chief clerks.

858. Do you mean graduated promotion when they become chief clerks?—No; but if the number of chief clerks could be increased. I don't see how they could be increased, but I consider that the two finance clerkships can only be filled satisfactorily by senior members of the staff, and it might be expedient therefore to place them on a scale of pay intermediate between that of the junior and the chief clerks.

859. Lord Monck.—If your office was vacant tomorrow, do you think there would be any difficulty in filling it from the rank of barristers of seven years' standing?—I should say not.

860. Mr. O'Reilly.—Do you think there would have been any difficulty in similarly filling it at the time the present scale of salaries was fixed, and at even a considerably less scale of salary than it was thought right and proper to be fixed at by the Treasury?—I think you would get parties to take the office at any salary.

861. Men that you would expect to be competent?—If you mean by competency, practice at the bar, I don't think any man of moderate practice would give it up to take the present salary—the man who has turned the corner, and is in fair practice, and who may look forward to further promotion. I know myself there are several men who would much prefer to get a chairmanship at £700 a year than get my office at at £1,000.

862. Is there any chairman so low as £700?—They commence at £700—£600, and £100 for registration.

Harry George Dixon, examined.

863. Lord Monck.—What position do you hold?—Junior clerk in the Metropolitan Police Court.

864. How long have you held that position?—Nine years and nine months.

865. What is your present actual rate of salary?—£130 a year.

866. When was your present scale of salary fixed—you have a salary beginning at £90, and increasing by £10 a year to £230?—That came into operation in 1870 only.

867. Have you any observation you would like to address to the Commissioners on your position?—With respect to that very point—as to the scale which was fixed in 1867 not coming into operation until 1870, I would wish to make an observation.

868. I may tell you the Commissioners do not think that is within the scope of their duty. That is a question for the Treasury, and you must apply to it; but if there is any other matter you would like to bring before us connected with your salary, we will

November 7.
—
Henry George Dixon

hear it ?—I would like to correct 'an opinion that Mr. Miller thought he left on the minds of the Commissioners which was erroneous, and that is, that the junior clerks in 1870 got an immediate rise of £30 a year for that year. That was not the case, for they did not all receive it; some had already passed the minimum of the new scale given at that time.

869. Have you any other points to bring under our consideration?—The want of promotion in the office, and the number of clerks in each class.

870. Do I understand your objection to be that eleven junior clerks is out of proportion to two senior?—Yes; out of proportion with that arrangement which exists in similar departments in London.

871. But, supposing the necessities of the service required only two chief clerks and eleven junior clerks, you would not propose, for the purpose of making promotion more rapid, that more chief clerks should be created?—Certainly not, for that purpose only.

Adjourned

November 21.
—
William Digges La Touche, esq.

NOVEMBER 21ST.

William Digges La Touche, esq., examined

872. Lord MONCK.—What position do you hold in the commercial world?—I am President of the Chamber of Commerce, a director of the Munster Bank, an agent of the Royal Exchange Insurance Company, and a director of the Dublin and Belfast Junction Railway. I am also a member of the Irish Railway Clearing House.

873. Let us take your own establishment, the Munster Bank—what number of clerks have you got there?—We have thirty-six or thirty-seven branches all through the country. I suppose we have upwards of 170 clerks.

874. What is the mode of appointment?—The mode of appointment is an examination in the ordinary rules of arithmetic and dictation, and plain history. It is not competitive. If the candidate rises to a certain standard we appoint him.

875. It is merely a pass examination?—Yes.

876 How are your clerks classified, or have you any general classification?—No, we have no general classification. Our only classification as to a rise in the bank, is according to their age and length of service. We have no classification as clerks. They are all considered the same.

877. They all do the same work?—Yes, they are all considered to do the same work.

878 At what rates do they enter the service?—They must be six months without salary, and if they are approved of then they get £20 for those six months, and on remaining six months more they get £20 more. That is £40 the first year, and afterwards they rise £10 a year until they come up to £100, provided that in the meantime they have not been promoted to some higher position than that of mere clerk. Up to seven years' service their promotion is absolute certainly, unless they are selected.

879. Unless they are selected. Then you do select them?—We do select them. We select the best men for a post such as accountant and cashier at a branch, or a book-keeper or teller. These are considered all the highest posts in the bank, and the manager of a branch is the highest of all. We pick out the best of the clerks for these things, and we advance their wages then by degrees. We do not give them a regular salary for a post, but we advance their salary by degrees, a little faster than they otherwise would be advanced if they had remained in their former position.

880. Would you tell us, beginning with the junior clerk, into what grades are the employés at the Munster Bank divided?—The junior clerk is merely used for copying and filing letters, and light duties about the office.

881. To what posts would a clerk be promoted?—Teller or accountant, cashier or book-keeper.

882. What are the salaries of these officers?—If we promote a man that had £100 a year, we give him £120 perhaps, and advance him then by degrees as he does his duties well to about £150. But we would not give him £150 at once, although we would consider £150 a salary fit for the post. We would not give a new hand the full salary at once.

883. Do I understand that when a man is promoted from the rank of clerk to one of those posts, you have him upon £150 a year?—Yes, ultimately.

884. Then a manager is the highest of his ambition?—Yes, there is a deputy manager in some of the more difficult branches. He is called the sub-manager, and he has a large salary.

885. What might his salary be?—It would be according to the branch. It would vary from £150 to £100 a year. The manager's salary would vary from £200 to £600, according to the importance of the branch. Of course, in such a case as the general manager in Cork, he has very much more.

886. Are the managers and the officers you have mentioned taken from the class of clerks?—Yes.

887. They all enter your service and rise?—In general, there have been instances of the contrary, where they have come to us from other banks as trained and experienced clerks, and when they do so, they are put in a position such as they occupied in the other bank.

888. But that is the exception?—Yes; we prefer our own boys.

889. Have you any difficulty in getting an adequate supply of well-qualified boys?—Not the least. The market is over-stocked altogether. There is a great number of applicants.

890. Mr. BLACKWOOD.—From what class of life would you say they are generally taken?—In general, they are merchants' sons, and sons of gentlemen and clergymen, and some few are shopkeepers' sons. Generally bankers' clerks are a higher class of young men.

891. Mr. O'REILLY.—How many posts of manager are there in your bank?—About thirty-six—as many as there are branches.

892. Then these posts are open to all the clerks?—Yes.

893. And they may look forward to promotion?—Yes, no matter what branch they are in they may look forward to promotion.

894. Mr. BLACKWOOD.—At what age do they generally enter the service of the bank?—At about seventeen. We prefer to take the boys at seventeen. Some of the other banks take them at nineteen, but we go as young as seventeen.

895. Do the rates of pay you have mentioned constitute the whole of their remuneration, or have they any allowance or advantage, such as house accommodation or anything of that kind?—The managers have houses, and the sub-managers sometimes, but the clerks have none.

896. Mr. O'REILLY.—Do you give any pensions?—No, no pensions. In case of very long service there have been instances, but they did not come under my notice, in which a sum of money has been given to the family.

897. But that is no part of the rule?—No.

898. What leave of absence do you give?—A fortnight in the year; that is the rule. There is one thing I have not mentioned, and that is, we require security of £1,000 from all our clerks.

899. About what other establishment with which you are connected could you give information?—If

you would take the Irish Railway Clearing-house, you would find it is very germane to the subject, employing as it does upwards of 100 clerks. The class of clerks there are very much the same as bankers' clerks, and their position is preparatory, in a great degree, to situations on the different railways. There is the same kind of examination, not competitive, but they must rise to a certain standard. They are taken in at £30 a year for the first year, except a month's probation, before they get upon the books. After the £30 salary, they rise £5 or £10 as they may deserve a year, until they come to £100. Then the heads of divisions—as they are called—may rise to £120 or £150 a year.

900. Mr. BLACKWOOD.—By what amount?—By £5 or £10 a year, except in peculiar cases where there is very good conduct, in which it might be made £15. They are a very good class of young men in the clearing-house. The business is very heavy, and requires a great deal of arithmetical calculation, worked most expeditiously. Therefore, they are a very fair class to go by.

901. Lord MONCK.—Is £100 a year the highest rate to which a clerk of the clearing-house can rise?—Yes, I think so; heads of departments rise as high as £300 a year.

902. Do the clerks in the clearing-house, as a rule, continue in the clearing-house for the period of their working lifetime?—I think in many instances they take the situation preparatory to railway or other employments, more than anything else. It is not looked upon so much as a profession as the bankers' clerks' position. At the same time a great number have been a long time there.

903. Have they any allowances?—No; except for extra work.

904. Their salary is their sole remuneration?—Yes.

905. And they have no pension?—No pension; but it is in contemplation to establish a superannuation fund.

906. And they have about the same leave of absence as they have in the bank?—Yes; I think we give them three weeks in the year.

907. Mr. BLACKWOOD.—Are they the same class of men generally as to social position?—A little lower in the scale than bankers' clerks, but not much. There is a great number of them quite the equal of bankers' clerks, but I think some of them are somewhat lower.

908. Lord MONCK.—Now will you take the insurance company?—Yes; the insurance companies take in very much the same class of boys as the bankers, I think entirely the same class.

909. At what age?—At the same age, about nineteen.

910. Is the age in the clearing-house about the same?—Yes; they take them into the clearing-house at seventeen years of age.

911. Have they to give any security in the clearing-house?—No; in the insurance offices they give them no salary the first year, and £50 the second year, and rise them arbitrarily. In insurance offices they merely rise when they become book-keepers and confidential clerks. They give them £50 or £60 a year until they get up sufficient knowledge to become confidential clerks. Then the salary varies up to £300 a year.

912. Between £150 and £200?—Yes.

913. And they cannot claim a rise?—No.

914. Mr. BLACKWOOD.—Have you many applications for clearing-house appointments and insurance companies' appointments?—A great number; quite as many as we want.

915. Lord MONCK.—Can you tell us whether any of these clerks in the different employments you have spoken of, ever enter the Government employment? Do they make the clearing-house or the banks a preparation for that?—Well, I think not. I do not know of any cases, except perhaps one or two, where they got Government employment.

916. Are you aware into what offices they went?—Some of them into the Castle; I do not know what departments. I know generally they were Government appointments.

917. You are also a director of the Belfast Junction

November 21.

William Digges La Touche, Esq.

Railway? Can you tell us the class of clerks and the rates of pay?—Almost the same class as bankers' clerks.

918. They are drawn from the same class?—Yes. We require boys at from seventeen to nineteen, to whom we pay about £40 a year during the first year, and we rise them gradually £10 a year until they have about £80.

919. Mr. BLACKWOOD.—Are these ticket-issuers?—No, merely clerks in the office. I am talking of the head office—the railways.

920. Not the stations?—No, not the stations.

921. Lord MONCK.—You were telling us £40 a year was the payment?—Yes, and they rise up to £80.

922. Not beyond that?—No, unless they get a post of head book-keeper or assistant clerk in the office.

923. What would their salaries be supposing they got there?—They would get up to £200 a year.

924. Can you tell us what the general traffic manager gets on your line?—I think in Ireland the salary would be from £500 to £1,000 a year.

925. And a house?—Yes, and a house.

926. As a rule have these traffic managers been taken from the subordinate clerks of the railway?—No.

927. Are these all the offices with which you are personally connected?—Yes. There is however another which I have known for many years, the office of the Grand Canal Company. That is a very old and respectable establishment, and we give a little higher salaries there. We take a boy up at £50 a year, and allow him to rise then—not yearly, but according as the directors think they are worthy of it, until they reach about £100. Then there are the positions of agents and station masters, where they may rise to £200 a year, and even to £350. Then in the office in Dublin there are posts in which a man may rise to £300 or £350 a year.

928. £350 a year is the highest point?—Yes.

929. Could you give us an idea what length of time it would take a man of ordinary intelligence and information to rise to that position?—It is gained by length of service and cleverness together. I suppose the ordinary run would be from ten to fifteen years' service.

930. Mr. BLACKWOOD.—What are the general hours of employment?—The banks are fixed—from half-past nine until half-past four. The banks close at three, but the clerks must stay there until the work is done. The insurance office is open from half-past nine until five o'clock, and in the clearing-house the hours are from ten until four.

931. And then in the Canal Company?—In the Canal Company the hours are from ten until five.

932. You said you were also a member of the Chamber of Commerce. Is there any establishment there?—There are very few clerks there; but I requested Mr. Bagot, the Honorary Secretary, to put upon paper a pretty good idea of what the commercial establishments of Dublin pay to their clerks. It is very much founded upon his own experience, but he told me he had consulted various merchants in Dublin, and the estimate is very much what the whole of them give. I put in his statement as part of my evidence. It is a pretty fair idea as far as my knowledge goes:—

MEMORANDUM OF SALARIES, &c., paid by WHOLESALE HOUSES in WINE, SPIRIT, and GENERAL BUSINESS, a fair guide in such concerns.

Traveller, No. 1.—Many years in the house; man of experience, £300 per year, and earns £60 by commission on sales—£360 per year.
Traveller, salary, £180; commission, £140—£320 per year.
Traveller, £101; £50 commission—£151 per year.
Book-keeper, £8 10s per month.
    Do.   £10 10s. per do.
    Do.   £8 10s. per do.
Assistant book keeper, young lad, £4 10s. per month.
    Do.   £3 per month.
General office clerk, £7 per month.
Head office assistant, £200 per year.
Custom House Clerk, £120 per year.
Cashier, £75 per year.

F 2

November 21.

William Digges La Touche, esq.

Young lad, £36 per year.

Do. £20 „

Do. £12 „

Yard clerk, 38s. per week.

Do. 21s. „

Apprentices not often taken; lads come in sometimes for first and second year without any pay. May get present at Christmas.

No examination; get respectable introduction; write a letter showing their handwriting and figures; attention, activity, and good conduct brings them on.

Generally gives leave of absence ten days to a fortnight when asked for, and in the dull season.

We have security for travellers; do not ask for it from others.

GROCERY TRADE.

Houses of best class give young men £40 to £80, sometimes £100, and head man £200 per year.

Second class, £20, and board; and lodging, to £30; and without board, £10, ranging to £70 and £90.

933. Have any of the institutions with which you are acquainted, or connected, branches in London or England?—No, we have no branches in England. The National Bank, who have a London branch, pay the same in London as in Dublin. I am informed that they give the same scale of salary in London as in Dublin.

934. Lord MONCK.—Is that regulated by the opinions you put before us to-day, or is it by the London scale?—No, I think they begin at £50 a year instead of £40. In the Hibernian Bank they begin at £50, as I have been told, and they go to £120 at the will of the directors. They have no fixed scale. I obtained from the Royal Bank their printed rules, of which the following is a copy:—

Rules made by the Directors of the ROYAL BANK of IRELAND, as to APPLICANTS for ADMISSION into the BANK'S SERVICE as PROBATIONERS.

1 Every applicant for admission into the bank's service must be at least fifteen years of age, must produce certificate of date of birth, must be free from bodily defect or infirmity, and must state so in his application.

2. Each applicant must be recommended by some person known to the directors or the principal officers of the bank, he must be of respectable connexions, and have had an education suitable to his condition in life, and be of unexceptionable conduct.

3. Each applicant must state, in a letter in his own handwriting, when and how he has been educated, his age, name, and profession of his father, if living, and his application should be accompanied by original testimonials.

4. Each applicant will be required to pass an examination before one of the bank's officers, and to appear before the directors.

5 Each probationer will be required to provide approved personal security, by the guarantee of two parties, for his good conduct and fidelity, to the extent of £300.

6. The term of probation is one year's service without salary; if found deserving after that period he will be placed on a salary of £40 per annum, and afterwards advanced as the directors may deem proper.

7. If, in the opinion of the directors, any probationer or clerk shall be found at any time to have misconducted himself in any respect, the directors may at any time dispense with his services without notice; in which case the officer or clerk so dismissed shall have no claim for salary or otherwise. He is not to quit the service of the bank without giving one month's notice, in writing, to the bank's secretary of his intention so to do. The directors may dispense with the services and terminate the engagement of any officer or clerk at any time, on giving him one month's notice of their intention to do so, and his salary will cease at the expiration of such notice.

You will see by that, that they do not rise by £10 a year, but at the will of the directors. They give nothing at all the first year. The following is the scale in the Provincial Bank:—

One year's probation, no salary; second year, £50; and afterwards generally rising to £100 by annual increases of £10—sometimes not so rapid, however—subsequent increases uncertain—both as to times and amounts—accountant and tellers at small branches range from £100 to £150. At large branches accountants' salaries vary from £140 or so to £250, which is the maximum. Managers commence generally at £250, and salaries range from that to £1,000, according to importance of branch.

935. Mr. BLACKWOOD.—Can you tell us how long those rates of pay have prevailed. Are they of long

standing, or have they been recently revised?—They have been recently revised in all with a rise. The bankers' clerks have been considered to be underpaid, and within the last two years their pay has been revised and raised. So far as I am aware of the feeling, and I am pretty well aware of it, we consider they are not sufficiently paid yet, and that we will have to rise them.

936. Lord MONCK.—Has there been any general complaint on the part of the clerks?—No; the supply is so large that they stay where they are.

937. The supply being so large and abundant for your purpose, what, may I ask, are the grounds upon which you think they are underpaid?—The prices of everything have risen to such an amount that the clerks may get into debt, and we think it better, for our own interest, to pay them a little more. I think it is under consideration and will be done as far as banks are concerned. I think the clerks are very much underpaid.

938. Have you formed any estimate in your own mind of the extent to which the salaries ought to be raised?—I think for the first year I would leave them as they are; but I would raise them the second and third year quicker than £10 a year. I would give them an increase of more than £10 a year for the second and third years, for a young man cannot live upon the smaller salary. He cannot live upon £50 or £60 the second or third year

939. Would you put the salary at £60 the first year?—No, I would pay £55 the second year and £70 the third, and then I would raise the salary by £10 a year.

940. Mr. BLACKWOOD.—Has the idea been entertained of adding a percentage to the salaries of all classes in consequence of the recent rise in the cost of living?—No; I think as far as banks are concerned we should never make a general rise in that way. We prefer keeping the matter in our own hands, and giving the increase to those who deserve it. We consider that the rate of salary ought to be higher, but we would not raise it by a percentage on all the clerks. We would not think of doing such a thing, as the increase would then go to the good men and the indifferent alike.

941. Lord MONCK.—But I understand that the ground on which you would increase the salary at present is not inefficiency of the individual, but his inability to live?—Yes.

942. Would not that apply to all clerks?—I think it would, but we should still have a right to withhold it, if a young man at the end of a year did not deserve it.

943. You would let him go about his business if he did not like it?—Yes

944. We have been dealing hitherto with clerks and persons of that class. Could you give us any information as to the remuneration given to inferior servants as porters in the railway, and in your own bank?—Yes; the railway porters are our masters at present, and it has been almost impossible to deal with them for the last two or three years. We have raised their wages exceedingly, and if we do not follow out their demands they just strike and leave us.

945 As I understand your answer, the difference between the two classes is, that of the clerks you have an abundant supply, and in the case of porters and subordinate officers, the supply is below the demand?—I would not say the supply is below the demand, because I think there are plenty of people to be had, but they are regulated by a society outside of us, and that society will not allow them to work under a certain rate. In fact we are not masters at all. The state of things at present is something terrible.

946. Could you give us a statement of the salary now given to men of that class—the men in your employment, in the different companies, who are inferior to the class of clerks?—Well, porters in the bank, for instance, get £1 a week.

947. And a house?—They live in the bank, and get coals and candles.

948. What are the qualifications of these men as regards literary acquirements?—They can all read and write.

949. Now, about the railway porters?—They generally average from 13s. to 18s. a week.

950. Mr. O'REILLY.—And clothes?—Yes.

951. Lord MONCK.—Are the qualifications of these men similar to those of bank porters?—They are not so high, but they almost all read and write. We do not take any that do not read and write.

952. Mr. BLACKWOOD.—I suppose as a general rule they would be younger men?—Yes; we want steady men at the bank.

953. Lord MONCK.—Can you give us any information as to the salaries of drivers, stokers, guards, and that class of men?—Our guards get from 18s. to 20s. a week.

954. They have no other advantages?—They have clothes. The drivers get 6s. to 7s. a day, or from 36s. to 42s. a week, some of them may even go up to 50s. a week. They get no clothes except a top-coat.

955. Mr. BLACKWOOD.—They are entitled to no pensions?—No.

956. Mr. O'REILLY.—But, as a matter of fact, do not the railway companies generally find situations that are less laborious which these men may occupy in their later years, such as gate-keepers?—Yes, we appoint them as gatemen, and send them to country stations where there is not so much work to do.

957. Mr. BLACKWOOD.—Have the railway company much difficulty in supplying the place of porters?—Indeed I think there is difficulty in it. It is very hard to get good men now.

958. Lord MONCK.—You have got in the railway company a large number of ordinary labourers?—Yes.

959. Are you aware what their pay is?—I think they get 13s. a week. The gangers get from 15s. a week up, and inspectors, 30s. to 36s. a week.

960. These men are what you would call unskilled labourers?—No, they are all skilled men.

961. In their particular line—but they are mere labourers?—Yes, but skilled in that particular work. Perhaps I may mention that the boatmen of the Grand Canal Company, and the Barrow Navigation, have had their pay increased in consequence of their having struck for higher wages. The masters of boats have been increased to £1 a week, and the second men to 18s. a week. They used to have 16s., and 17s. per week.

962. What is the character of the work they perform?—They navigate the boats along the canal, and take charge of the whole cargo. There is a good deal of trust about their situations, but they are not a high class of men in any way.

963. Do you employ on the railways, or in any of the companies with which you are connected, any men of the artisan class, such as masons and carpenters?—In the locomotive department we have skilled artisans.

These men get very high wages. They get from 26s. to £2 a week.

964. Where is your locomotive department situated?—In Dundalk.

965. Do you imagine that that is the ordinary rate of wages for men of that class in the neighbourhood of Dundalk?—Yes.

966. You have no reason to believe these are picked men?—No; for on all the railways they are pretty much the same. In fact, they go from one company to another. At the Grand Canal we employ a number of carpenters and smiths, and the wages are from 30s. to £2 for carpenters—boat builders they are called—who are engaged in repairing boats.

967. Can you give us any idea of the increased cost of living in Dublin within the last five or ten years?—I can give you some idea of it, because I have to pay for it. There is no doubt it has increased greatly. We are paying 10d. and 11d. a pound for meat, and I remember when we could get it at from 5d. to 6d. a pound.

968. Can you fix any date for that?—I dare say fifteen years ago. I think it has been gradually rising for ten years up to the point at which it is. Ten years ago it was certainly 5d. or 6d. a pound.

969. Could you give us, from your own personal expenditure, a statement of the rates at which you purchased the following articles in 1862, and what you are paying for them now:—Beef, mutton, bacon, milk, eggs, butter, and bread?—

	1862.	1872.
Mutton, per lb.,	7d.	10½d.
Roasting beef, per lb.,	7d.	11d.
Boiling beef, per lb.,	6d.	8d.
Bacon, per lb.,	8½d.	9½d.
Milk, per quart,	3d.	4d.
Eggs, per doz.,	10d.	1s. 2d.
Butter, per lb.,	1s. 4d.	1s. 7d.
Bread, per 2 lb. loaf,	4½d.	4½d.

970. Mr. BLACKWOOD.—Do you think that house-rent has increased in Dublin?—No, I think not.

971. Is the rent of the class of houses which are occupied by the clerks in the different establishments to which you have referred increased?—I think not. There has been a great number of additional houses built in the suburbs of Dublin, and I think the rents are as cheap as they ever were. Tea, sugar, and coffee are cheaper than they ever were.

972. Would you say that servants' wages have increased?—Yes, I think they have, but not as much, except for the higher class of servants.

973. Not for maid-servants?—Not so much for the lower class of servants. I wish to express my strong conviction that the bankers' clerks, as a class, are underpaid in Dublin and the country..

James C. Colvill, esq., examined.

974. Lord MONCK.—You are Governor of the Bank of Ireland?—I am.

975. Are your clerks in the bank divided into classes?—As regards salaries?

976. Yes?—Originally they were, but they are not now.

977. How are they appointed?—By examination. That system is of recent origin; perhaps for some eight or ten years we have had an examination held at the bank, at which the candidates were first examined, and then we made a selection from amongst the best qualified.

978. Is the examination competitive?—It is competitive now, but was not originally. Originally it was an examination more for qualification; and after the examination the directors had a committee of selection, which went through the returns, and selected the men they thought best; but two or three years ago there was some dissatisfaction with that system, because a candidate might say, no matter even if he answered best, he was not selected. We then altered our system and substituted a regular competitive examination. We reversed the order of procedure. We first had the committee of selection, and then the examination,

which was purely competitive, and the best man passed. We still retained the selection, because we did not consider a man's answering was conclusive proof that he was the man we wanted. I have in my possession one of our printed forms about our examination, which perhaps may be interesting, as showing how it is carried out.

979. Will you put that in?—Yes. I may mention that formerly the examiners were some of the heads of our departments. That did not give satisfaction, and now our examinations are carried on by two of the Fellows of Trinity College, and they generally bring in some other gentleman—Mr. Hancock, for instance—who is connected with one of the insurance companies, for book-keeping, but the examination is now, you may say, conducted by two Fellows of Trinity College, so that there shall be no idea of partiality. [The witness handed in the following document.]—

RULES FOR ELECTION OF CLERKS, BANK OF IRELAND, 1872.

Bank clerkships shall be of the annual value on entrance of £60, increasing (for clerks continuing in the service of the bank) to £100 by annual increments of £8. Further

November 21.

James C.
Colvill, esq.

increase being thenceforth dependent on the position which the zeal and ability of each gentleman may, in the estimation of the Board of Directors, entitle him to fill, and subject to the regulations as to security, nature, and sphere of duty, from time to time directed by the Board.

Candidates must obtain a nomination from a member of the Board of Directors, each director, including the governor and deputy governor, to have five nominations. Candidates to be not less than seventeen years, and not more than twenty-five years of age, at time of appearing before a committee of selection. Nominations to be in force for the then next election only; any unsuccessful candidate desiring to compete again, to provide himself with a fresh nomination.

Candidates so nominated shall appear before the committee of selection, who shall have power to reject such of them as may be considered unsuited in any way for the service of the bank.

Candidates approved of by the committee of selection shall procure, at their own cost, a medical certificate from some one of the doctors to be named by the bank, on a form to be procured from the secretary, certifying their soundness of health and constitution, and shall then be tested by a competitive examination, to be held at such time, in such place, and subject to such rules, as the Board of Directors shall from time to time lay down; such examination to be carried on by examiners unconnected with the bank, and as far as practicable by papers, the candidates competing by a number, and not by name. Those candidates who shall have received in the aggregate of subjects the largest number of marks shall be elected to the appointments then offered for competition, provided that the number of marks in each subject shall reach the minimum fixed as a standard of qualification.

The subjects for examination shall be as follow:—

	Maximum.	Minimum.
1. Handwriting,	500	400
2. Arithmetic,	500	300
3. Orthography, Dictation,	500	400
4. Book-keeping,	300	100
5. English History and Geography,	300	80
6. Algebra (to quadratic equations),	300	—

980. Lord Monck.—I see by this paper that the minimum rate of pay is £60 a year?—£60 a year for juniors, and they rise by an increment of £8 a year, up to £100; in five years they have £100.

981. Mr. Blackwood.—At what age do they enter?—From 17 to 25.

982. Lord Monck.—Are the higher appointments in the bank all made by selection from those clerks who enter at £60?—Generally; we do not bind ourselves, but as a general rule they are. If we have a fit man in the bank we give him promotion.

983. What are the duties of these clerks from £60 to £100 a year?—They generally enter either as juniors in some of the country branches, or in the book-keeper's office; that office is, in fact, a sort of draw farm; they all go in there to learn something of business, and are taken from that into the other parts of the establishment as they are fit and are wanted.

984. What would be the promotion which these clerks could look forward to, and what would be their next step?—There are the country establishments which have now become the largest, and there is the town establishment. In the country establishments they enter as juniors, and their next step is to become a cashier, the next sub-agent, and then from that they become an agent.

985. That is the course of promotion in the county districts?—In the country establishments.

986. What is it in the town establishment?—In the town they enter as juniors generally in the book-keeper's office, in the transfer office or dividend office; then their next step is either to get into the secretaries' office, the agent's office, or into the cash office. In the secretaries' office they always have higher pay; there is no junior in the secretaries' office under £80 a year, no matter what his standing is. If he goes into the secretaries' office after one year's service he at once goes up to £80 a year; they are kept till later hours, and it is a better class of work, and the same way in the agent's office.

987. The agent's office is the same?—The same. They go up to £80 a year at once, when they get in there.

988. Well then, the cash office?—The cash office is rather exceptional in that way; there is not much promotion for a man until he becomes a teller, and then the advance in his salary is very considerable.

989. We'll take the offices one by one. The junior goes into the book-keeper's or transfer office?—Yes; they are promoted from that to the secretaries', the agent's, or the cash office.

990. We'll take the secretaries' office first. When a man gets into the secretaries' office at a salary of £80, or a higher rate of salary, what would be his next step?—There are two gradations of men in the secretaries' office, not far divided until they get to some of the higher duties, or become assistant-secretaries.

991. And with larger salaries?—With considerably larger salaries.

992. What are the salaries in the secretaries' office?—The salaries range, they begin at £80; there are gentlemen who have £100, £130, £160, and £300; the assistant-secretary I think has £600, and the secretary himself has £1,000 a year.

993. Have you more than one assistant-secretary?—No.

994. Now, let us take the agency office. What would be the gradation of salary there?—They get in at £80 or £100. Then, perhaps, there are not so many gradations. There is an outer office and an inner office, and the men in the outer office have from £30 to perhaps £120 a year, and then there are three superior men in the inner office. There is the inspector of branches £1,000 a year, his assistant has £300 a year, and the man next to him has about £300 a year.

995. How many men have you got in the secretary's office altogether?—I think about twelve; twelve or fourteen.

996. And in the agency office?—In the agency office there are probably more. There are twenty-five.

997. The cash office is the other you have mentioned?—In the cash office, when a man is appointed a teller—we have three gradations of tellers—he begins at about £100 a year; he has £45 a year risk money. He is always required to keep one year's risk money on hand, which is counted as his money—it is put on deposit receipt; but in case of his making any mistake we always require him to keep one year's risk money. We keep it in hand for him—we pay him interest on it, and it is his money; but he has that in addition to his salary.

998. Is it not security?—No.

999. Then the second gradation of tellers?—The salary is £126, and the same risk money; and the highest teller has £150 and his risk money.

1000. What number of men are there in the cash office?—Altogether there are in the cash department fifty.

1001. Will you tell us in round numbers how many junior clerks there are in addition to these?—You have told us how many in the book-keeper's and transfer offices?—We have altogether in Dublin 180 in round numbers, and of these I suppose fifty or sixty are what we call junior clerks.

1002. What is the salary of the cashier in the country?—We have no cashier in the country under £100 a year, and they rise according to the amount of business in the office and the amount of duty they have to perform. They range from £100 a year up to £300 a year; in some of our large provincial towns there are one or two tellers. Our head teller in Cork has £160 a year, and in Belfast our head teller has £160 a year. They have not been very long appointed.

1003. Then the sub-agents?—The sub-agents are from about £160 a year up to £400 a year.

1004. And the agents?—The agents run from £700 a year up to £1,000. We have only one agent with £1,000 a year, in Belfast, in Cork he has £800 a year; in Limerick, Waterford, and Newry, and other large towns they have £600 a year.

1005. Mr. O'Reilly.—Have they apartments?—

They have house, servant, and coals, and all that in the bank.

1006. Lord MONCK.—Have the sub-agents?—In many places the sub-agents have accommodation at the banks. We have built houses large enough to give them.

1007. And the cashiers?—The cashiers have no accommodation. Our chief cashier and deputy cashier have a house in Dublin. They live in the bank.

1008. Are these the only officers of the bank that have accommodation?—The secretary has a house, and the two cashiers, and the head of the transfer department who is also called the house-keeper; he has the care of the house.

1009. Can you tell us what is the number of your country employés?—About 200.

1010. Two hundred in the country and 150 in Dublin?—Yes; we have forty-five branches

1011. Do any of the persons in your employment give security?—Yes, for the first three years they have to find security—their personal security, or we take in some cases the guarantee society.

1012. Then after three years?—They come on the guarantee fund of the house.

1013. Mr. BLACKWOOD.—Do they contribute to that fund?—They contribute to it.

1014. Lord MONCK.—What is their contribution?—In Dublin heads of departments give security for £3,000. They pay, by quarterly instalments, £16 in three years; and the next security is £2,000 for a cashier, and he has to pay £12 in three years, and then the junior clerk is to give £1,000 security, and he pays £8 in three years. At the branches agents give £4,000 security, and their subscription is £20, sub-agents, £3,000, subscription £16; cashiers, £3,000, subscription £12, junior clerks, £1,000, subscription £8, all payable by quarterly instalments in three years.

1015. In three years?—In three years.

1016. And nothing after that?—Yes, after that if there is a loss made, they have to begin to contribute over again until the loss is made good, so that a certain sum of money must be always kept to the credit of the fund, and the moment that is reduced they have all to begin to contribute again.

1017. The whole of the establishment?—Yes.

1018. Do you give any pensions?—We have three funds in our bank—an annuity fund, an education fund, and an insurance fund, but they are all supported by the bank independent of the clerks; an annuity fund for our widows after seven years—men who have been seven years in the establishment. They run from seven years, then adding five, twelve, seventeen, and twenty-two years, and in the same way they begin at £25 a year and go up to £40 Irish currency.

1019. Twenty-five pounds is the minimum annuity, and £40 is the maximum?—Quite so.

1020. And that annuity must be obtained on retirement?—No; that is merely for the man's widow.

1021. It is a widow's annuity?—A widow's annuity. Then there is the education fund For children between five and fifteen there is £12 a year given no matter of what standing the man is.

1022. On his death?—On his death, for the education of his children.

1023. And the insurance?—The insurance we established two years ago The Board undertook to pay half the premium for any man who chose to insure his life up to the amount of £300. We pay half the premium. It is only just beginning to work now.

1024. Are these three funds maintained by the bank irrespective of any contribution on the part of men?—They are with this single exception, that any fines that are levied for irregular attendance are thrown into the education fund. They amount to a mere bagatelle, £30 or £40 a year. We are now paying £1,745 per annum annuities, and £336 per annum for education, and though we have no scale for superannuations we are now paying about £3,600 per annum under that head, and for insurance £600 per annum.

1025. There is no reduction?—There is no reduction from salaries.

1026. I understand you that, irrespective of these funds, and the allowance of house and coals, the salaries of the persons in your employment are the sole remuneration for their services?—No, they have an opportunity of earning from what is called extra work; that is, working after regular bank hours. Some of the men earn from £10 to £40, and over £50 a year for extra work, which cannot well be done during bank hours. They come earlier in the morning, or stay in the evening.

1027. What are the bank hours?—Half-past nine in the morning to about four o'clock. As I mentioned before, in the secretaries' offices they have to remain later, perhaps five.

1028. Has there been of late years any increase in the pay of your clerks?—Yes, decidedly. A few years ago a junior clerk entered at £60 a year, and at the end of one year he was raised £10, but got no further advance whatever for six years, but now he goes up to £100 in five years, independent of the chance he has, if he is a smart fellow, of getting on better.

1029. The promotions we have been speaking of take place entirely by selection?—Yes, we go every half-year through our whole establishments, both in town and country, and revise salaries and promotions.

1030. Do the men who engage with you as junior clerks, as a general rule, make your employment their profession?—I think so; in fact, we make it a sine quâ non in the first instance, when they present themselves for examination, that they propose to make the bank their profession We won't allow any man to be a student of college, because we found the bad effects of it.

1031. Then as a matter of fact men do not prepare themselves in your establishment, and go into Government or other employment from it?—No, I think not.

1032. Mr. BLACKWOOD.—From what class of society are the clerks in your bank generally taken?—There has been a change in that respect in the last few years. Since we began the competitive examinations we have had a much greater variety of men tendering themselves, but before that, I think they were generally from a higher grade of society than they are now.

1033. Although you have raised the qualification?—Although we have raised the qualification and pay; but I should say even now the great majority of the men in our service are gentlemen by birth and connexions.

1034. Have you any difficulty in obtaining candidates for employment?—Yes; much more than we used to have. Before the competitive examinations we generally had 130 candidates on our books, and a great deal of interest was made to get them into the bank. At the first competitive examination we had but ninety; our next competitive examination we had to adjourn for a month, we had only thirty candidates, and after adjourning it for a month, we had only about forty-seven who presented themselves. Of these the committee of selection rejected five or six, and only forty came up to the test.

1035. Lord MONCK.—How many vacancies were there?—But twelve.

1036. And forty candidates?—Yes.

1037. Mr. O'REILLY.—Of the forty men who presented themselves for examination, how many did you consider came up to the standard of qualification which you would expect in your clerks?—Eight. Eight were fully qualified. There were four who were disqualified on two subjects, but their aggregate marks were more than some of the eight, and as we really wanted the hands we took those four in.

1038. Lord MONCK.—That was in '71?—No; the other day; in fact this month.

1039. Mr. BLACKWOOD.—Do you think that tends to show that the rate of remuneration offered by the bank is insufficient to attract men of the required qualification?—It is very hard to say. Really our standard of education is not above what any person educated in the National schools ought to come up to.

November 21.

James C. Colvill, esq.

1040. Lord MONCK.—The bearing of Mr. Blackwood's question is this—do you attribute the paucity of candidates to the insufficiency of the remuneration or the scarcity of the class?—I should attribute it to the scarcity of the class of persons.

1041. You are aware within the last two or three years entrance into the Civil Service has been opened to general competitive examination?—Yes.

1042. Do you think that may have an effect on the numbers coming to you?—I do. I was going to add to the answer I gave that I think the two things hang together very much. I think that any young man who has any sort of energy goes to other places and other departments where he is better paid; and hence in this country we have not the number of persons who are satisfied with the employment they can get here. I know in mercantile life there is a great deal of employment in London, and Liverpool, and other places I have business communications with; and any man who is really worth anything can get his £200 and £300 a year in an office just as easily as he can get half the money here. These is no doubt about it.

1043. Mr. O'REILLY.—Do you think £200 or £300 a year at the opposite side of the channel attracts Irishmen in preference to half the money here?—No doubt of it; a man can live as cheaply if not more cheaply and better in some of the larger cities of England than he can here.

1044. Lord MONCK.—You have just said you are acquainted with the rates of remuneration paid by mercantile houses in Liverpool?—Yes.

1045. Could you give us any comparative estimate of what is paid to the same class here and in Liverpool?—That opens a difficult question, because you must judge of the value of the article. There is more business doing there, and any sharp hand, a really good intelligent man, will bring money that he never would have obtained here, because the field is so much smaller, and the amount of business doing does not admit of men paying the salaries that men can afford to pay in England. I know men who have gone over from this to Liverpool—I am speaking now of a few years ago, who perhaps had £100 a year in a merchant's office, and after perhaps a couple of years, being found to be smart, intelligent fellows, got £300 a year. If they remained here they would never, at least in these days, receive that, because men cannot afford to pay their clerks in that way. They are satisfied with an inferior article at a lower salary.

1046. Then your opinion is that the extent of the business transacted by mercantile firms in England, enables them to give salaries which the transactions in Ireland could not afford, and thereby attracts to England the best talent of the Irish intelligence market, so to speak?—No doubt; I think it is a very simple conclusion.

1047. Mr. BLACKWOOD.—Do you consider at the same time the duties of the bank are efficiently performed by the officers whom you are now able to obtain?—I think so, I don't mean to say they could not be better done.

1048. Lord MONCK.—Can you give us any measure of the increase of salary which has been given to the people in the employment of the bank within the last two or three years?—I can within these two years, because I have been looking into it, and, with a very few exceptions where it was not merited, and others where advances had been recently granted, in no case have we given less than six per cent. advance, and not a few men have got advances—I am now putting promotion out of the question, but advances in salary while in the same position—up to I should say thirty-five per cent., and in a few cases over fifty per cent.; and the increase in the two years (including promotions) to the same individuals, between June, 1870, and June, 1872, has been fully £7,500.

1049. We have been talking hitherto of the clerks and superior employees in the bank, can you give us any account of the salaries paid to inferior men—to porters, and people of that class?—Yes, we have a good many, and we have increased the salaries of all that class of men I should say fully 15 per cent.

1050. Within what period?—Within the last two years.

1051. What is the present rate of salary of the porters in the bank?—I think now we have got no man under a pound a week, and they go from that up to 30s. a week, and they have clothes. They have no house accomodation, or anything of that kind.

1052. What qualifications do you require in men of that class—I mean literary qualifications?—In fact none.

1053. Don't you insist on their being able to read and write?—Read and write, that is all.

1054. Could you give us any information as to the remuneration in any other large establishment in Dublin?—There is one it occurs to me you might ask me about, the Port and Docks Board. As I was passing now I just refreshed my mind about the salaries there. It is a small establishment, and, you may say, has been only recently formed. The secretary of that establishment has now £600 a year, rising by annual increment of £50 to £750, the bookkeeper has £250, rising by £10 to £300, and the cashier, £160, rising by £10 to £200, and two junior clerks in the office are taken in at £80, and rise by £10 to £130. Now even in that establishment there has been an advance in the short period since the period it was separated from the Lighthouse Board. Then in connexion with the Port and Docks Board there is the establishment of the Custom-house Docks. There are a great number of persons, labourers and warehousemen employed in them, and a considerable advance in their wages has taken place within the last two years.

1055. Could you tell us what the general rate of increase of wages in the warehousing is?—I think within the last two years more labourers' wages have risen from 15s. up to 18s. a week, and warehousemen from 30s. to 32s. 6d. per week.

1056. And these are more labourers?—Mere labourers and warehouse people. In fact the labour market here, particularly in Dublin, is very considerably advanced.

1057. You reside in Dublin?—Yes.

1058. You are aware the cost of living has increased very much within the last few years?—Yes.

1059. Could you give us from your own experience a statement of the price of different articles of consumption now and ten years ago?—I could easily do so.

1060. We want to get the price of beef, mutton, bacon, milk, eggs, butter, bread, tea, sugar, and coffee?—   If instead of ten you were to take ten and twenty, I think the results would be much more startling. I have no doubt about that, because really compared with twenty years ago the difference in meat is 100 per cent. Twenty years ago £100 a year to a person was very nearly as good to him as £200, if he was transplanted to Liverpool, or any of these places, but now that is altered, and in fact the value of living is a float level between the two countries.*

Adjourned.

*Date.	Beef, per lb.			Mutton, per lb.	Fowl, per couple.	Bacon, per lb.	Coal, per ton.	Milk, per quart.	Eggs, per doz.	Butter, per lb.	Bread, per lb.	Tea, per lb.	Coffee, per lb.	Sugar, per lb.
	Prime.	Salt.	Soup.											
1872, .	10d.	8d.	4½d.	9½d.–8½d.	4s.	10d.–9d.	Exceptional.	4d.	1s. 8d.	1s. 8d.	2½d.	3s.–3s. 10d.	1s. 6d.	4d.–6d.
1862, .	7½d.	6½d.	3½d.	7d.–4d.	3s.	8d.–7d.	14s.–15s.	3d.	1s.	1s. 2d.	—	3s. 10d.	—	—
1852, .	6d.	5d.	3½d.	6d.–4d.	2s. 6d.	6d.–5d.	12s.–14s.	2½d.	7d.	1s.	1½d.	4s.	—	—

APPENDIX.

DUBLIN METROPOLITAN POLICE.

APPENDIX I.

REPORT of the CHIEF COMMISSIONER to GOVERNMENT.

Metropolitan Police Office, Dublin Castle.
26th March, 1872.

The Chief Commissioner of Police feels it his duty to bring to the notice of Government the very great discontent which has lately been evinced by the members of the force under his command, at the smallness of the pay they receive, compared to that enjoyed by the several Police services in England.

This feeling of dissatisfaction has shown itself in many ways, not only through the medium of letters written to the Dublin Press, and published in various newspapers from time to time, but in the more certain and tangible form of a very largely increased number of resignations continually sent in on the plea of insufficiency of pay, and the late reduction in the amount of pension.

Before submitting any remarks on this most important case, the Commissioner considered it absolutely necessary to satisfy himself as to the grounds which exist for this discontent on the part of the Metropolitan Police, and he takes the liberty of laying before Government the result of his inquiries.

When the Dublin Metropolitan Police were first established, it is an undoubted fact that provisions and all the necessaries of life could be procured at a rate of at least a third cheaper than what the same articles can be purchased for at the present time, and yet the pay of the force, it may be truly said, has not been increased to meet the necessities of the times, while in every Police force in England the pay has been gradually getting larger, until it has assumed a very great disproportion to that of the Dublin force. The consequence naturally is, that many men, after two or three years' service—remaining just long enough to establish their characters—have sent in their resignations, and gone over to the London, Liverpool, and other Police forces. Many young men, also, who have only joined a few weeks or months, have applied for permission to leave the service, on the plea of finding the pay so small that they were unwilling to continue in it, when they knew well that they could obtain higher wages elsewhere.

It is quite true that so long as the prospect of considerable pensions was held out to the men, they were willing to toil on, receiving their limited pay with the certainty that if they lived they would obtain a competency in their declining years.

This, and this alone, induced many men to continue in the force, and this prospect will no doubt prevent the force losing any man of a certain standing; but the question to be looked at is—How is the force to be now recruited and kept up in its hitherto efficient state?

The Commissioner would beg leave to direct attention to the Table marked A, annexed, by which is will be seen that during the year ending the 1st March, 1872, 179 men have resigned and been removed, either from ill health or other causes, while the number of enlistments has amounted to only 107.

There was a time, not long after the Commissioner joined the service, in 1868, when he had a list of approved candidates amounting to sometimes as many as a hundred, who had passed all the necessary tests, and who then proceeded to their respective homes, eagerly awaiting the time when they would be called upon to serve; whereas at the present moment, in lieu of having 40 recruits at the Depot, the authorised number, there are but three. Moreover, he may have remark that the style of the present recruit is widely different from what it was some few years ago, and instead of the tall, stalwart, well-educated man who formerly joined the Metropolitan Police, a very inferior class now present themselves, both as regards physique and intelligence, and much time is lost by having to keep them for a longer period at the Depot. An experiment was made at one time by taking recruits below the minimum standard, which had

from the formation of the force been so rigidly kept up, and which had justly obtained for the Dublin Metropolitan Police the name of the finest force in the United Kingdom; but the experiment totally failed, and of late scarcely any candidates have presented themselves.

When the difference in the rate of pay between the Dublin Police and that of other similar forces is considered, and the little difference which really exists in the expense of living, it can scarcely be wondered at that discontent has begun to show itself, more particularly when the rate of labour of a certain class in Dublin is also taken into consideration. For instance, the mason porters, who receive 27s. a week for six or seven hours' labour, without incurring the same risk of life, or undergoing any of the hardships which a constable on his beat is hourly and nightly exposed to.

It is true the pensions to which the police may look forward, if they live long enough, and conduct themselves properly, are a great inducement to men to enter the force, but by an Act passed in 1867 (vide Table marked B) the pensions are considerably reduced, and thus the prospects of the men now joining, and of those who have joined since the said year, are far worse than those of their seniors in the service.

The annexed documents marked C, D, E, and F show respectively the rates of pay of the London Metropolitan Police, the Manchester, the Liverpool, the Stafford, and Chester Police Forces.

In dealing with his subject, however, the Commissioner will only take the London Force as being the one which alone resembles that of Dublin, being independent of a corporation, and the two forces being formed on the same model.

He may observe that an approved candidate for the Dublin Metropolitan Police, during the period he is in the Depot receiving instruction in drill and police duty, is called a supernumerary, and he receives only ten shillings per week during that period, which at an average is four months.

On his appointment as constable he is placed on the fourth rate and receives 15s. 6d. per week, the corresponding grade in London receiving 20s. In the course of time he becomes third rate and receives 16s. 9d. per week, the corresponding grade in London receiving 23s. per week; then second rate at 17s. 6d. per week, the corresponding grade in London receiving 24s.; and then, first rate at 18s. per week, the corresponding grade in London receiving 26s. On an average constables arrive at first rate in Dublin and also in London after having served eight years, yet the pay of the first-rate constable in London is equal to the pay of an acting inspector or station sergeant in Dublin, a grade which is always attained by competition, and rarely before fifteen years have been spent in the service.

In Dublin only constables on first rate are eligible to compete for acting sergeant, and if a man be qualified after ten or twelve years' service he may hope to be promoted acting sergeant at 20s. per week (the pay of the fourth rate or lowest grade in London), the corresponding grade in London being 26s., he may then become sergeant and receive 23s. per week the corresponding grade of first-class ordinary sergeant in London receiving 31s. per week; then acting inspector at 26s. per week, the corresponding grade of station sergeant in London receiving 35s. Clerk sergeants in Dublin receive only 25s. per week as ordinary sergeants, but in London they receive 35s. per week.

The Commissioner will not at present pursue this comparison further than to remark that in the G, or Detective, Division in Dublin, formed on the London system at Scotland-yard, there are constables at 16s. and 20s. per week, acting sergeants at 22s. per week, sergeants at 25s. per week, acting inspectors at 27s. 6d. and 30s. 6d. per week, and inspectors at £135 per year, and a superintendent at £310 per year, who has also important duties in connexion with the hackney vehicles to discharge, while the detective department in Scotland-yard consists of sergeants at 42s. and 57s. 6d. per week, inspectors at £200 per year each, and chief inspectors at £300 per year each, and a superintendent at £350 per year, and the auxiliary detectives, constables, and sergeants in London receive 36s. and 33s. per week respectively.

But although comparison has been made with London it does not appear that the highest rate of Police wages is paid there, or that Police wages in Dublin are on an equality with any county or borough in England, the contrary generally being the case.

At A. in the extract from Report on Liverpool Police,* it is stated that the average wages paid to constables of the lowest grade in eight large towns in England is 19s. 10½d. per week, or 4s. 4½d. per week more than the lowest, and over 10½d. per week more than the highest in Dublin, the average highest rate being 23s. 6d. per week, or 6s. 6d. per week more than the highest, and 10s. a week more than the lowest in Dublin.

The cost of living and price of labour are at present as high in Dublin as in any English town, and a man can reach Liverpool or Manchester as cheaply as Dublin from other parts of Ireland. Bills from Newcastle-on-Tyne were sent to Police Stations in Dublin (see that marked G), also from Salford and Chester, soliciting candidates, and the Commissioner of Police has no doubt that many of the constables who have voluntarily resigned the Dublin Police have joined, or will join, those other Police Forces where the pay is so much better.

The fear is that these very men, finding their prospects so much improved, may write and induce their comrades in Dublin to follow their example, and thus, taking into consideration the paucity of candidates who now present themselves, and the still smaller number who will come as soon harvest time begins, there is every prospect of such a diminution taking place in the strength of the force as to render it impossible to carry on the duties satisfactorily, unless something be immediately done to ameliorate their condition, and put a stop to the resignations now daily coming in. The report of the number of resignations is made up to 1st March, 1872, but since that date more men (7) have resigned.

The vacancies now in the force amount to 60, including supernumeraries, there being only three supernumeraries at the Depôt.

The force, if at its full authorized strength, is barely sufficient to carry out its duties when deduction is made for non-effectives connected with its own interior economy, together with the many and daily increasing demands from other departments. At present the suburbs of the metropolis, of the adjacent towns, and the roads in the extensive suburbs, are not properly patrolled. Should the resignations continue, the Commissioner fails to see how the duties can be carried on, and with still further reduced numbers it will be impossible to give through the metropolitan districts that amount of protection to life and property which has hitherto been expected and enjoyed by the citizens.

The Commissioner has endeavoured, as briefly as possible, and without entering into unnecessary details, to lay before Government, as he feels in duty bound to do, the present state of the Dublin Police Force, setting forth the nature of the complaints made by its members, and what he ventures to consider their just grounds for the same. He has delayed drawing out and submitting to Government a report on this subject, hoping that the discontent among the members of the Metropolitan Police might happily pass away; but such has not been the case, and he is convinced that he should no longer feel justified in withholding from Government facts which, if not speedily remedied, may possibly lead to serious consequences, involving the permanent impairment of the value of the service, now for thirty-six years the freely-admitted protective force of the metropolis.

The Commissioner of Police will only observe in conclusion, that should Government be pleased to take steps for improving the condition of the Dublin Metropolitan Police, there is every reason to believe that the citizens are quite prepared to do their part in assisting to effect an object so immediately conducive to the public interests.

HENRY ATWELL LAKE.

The Under Secretary. &c.

[RETURN.

* See enclosure marked E.

A.

3rd March, 1872.

RETURN showing the number of Men who Joined the Dublin Metropolitan Police, from 1st March, 1871, to the present date, the number of those who Resigned voluntarily, the number who were Dismissed, the number who were Discharged from Ill-health, and the number who Died while serving.

	Joined.	Superannuated.	Constables.	Dismissed by Commissioner.	Discharged for Ill Health.	Dead.
1871.						
March,	9	..	3	1	8	..
April,	10	6	6	5	2	..
May,	8	6	6	7	..	..
June,	13	4	3	1	4	..
July,	11	..	2	1	..	..
August,	7	3	1	4	3	1
September,	14	..	3	1	1	..
October,	9	3	3	3	1	3
November,	8	2	3	3	1	3
December,	8	1	3	5	6	..
1872.						
January,	7	1	8	3	3	2
February,	8	2	6	2	8	..
March,	4	1	6	3	..	2
Total,	**107**	**26**	**51**	**39**	**18**	**11**

Total number of Men who joined, . . . 107
  „ „ all removals, . . . 173

B.

DUBLIN METROPOLITAN POLICE SUPERANNUATION ACTS:
10 & 11 Vic., cap 100.

SCALE for Men appointed before the Act was passed in 1847, viz.:—

After 15 and under 20 years' service, . Two-thirds of pay.
After 20 years' service, ... Full pay.

Appointments after the Act.

Above 15 and under 20 years, . Half of pay.
  „ 20 „ „ 25 „ . Two-thirds of pay.
  „ 25 „ „ 30 „ . Three-fourths of pay.
After 30 years' service, . . . Full pay.

30 & 31 Vic., cap. 95. 1867.

15 years' service, pension of fifteen-fiftieths.
One-fiftieth increase for each succeeding year up to 30 years.
After 30 years, or when 60 years of age, thirty-fiftieths, or a larger sum, in cases of extraordinary merit.

C.

March, 1872.

RETURN showing the Rates of Pay of the various Grades in the Dublin Metropolitan Police, also the Pay of the corresponding Grades in the London Metropolitan Police, for comparison, to show the Excess of Pay in London over the Pay in Dublin.

	DUBLIN.			LONDON.			
	£	s.	d.		£	s.	d.	
Supernumerary,	0	10	0	per week.	—			per week.
4th-rate Constable,	0	16	8	„	1	0	0	„
3rd-rate „	0	16	3	„	1	3	0	„
2nd-rate „	0	17	6	„	1	4	0	„
1st-rate „	0	19	0	„	1	6	0	„
Acting-Sergeant,	1	0	0	„	1	9	0	„
Full „	1	5	0	„	1	11	0	„
Clerk „	1	5	0	„	1	15	0	„
Acting-Inspector,	1	6	0	„	1	15	0	„
3rd-class „	107	0	0	per year.	118	12	6	per year.
2nd-class „	115	0	0	„	136	17	4	„
1st-class „	122	0	0	„	164	5	0	„
Superintendent (minimum),	180	0	0	„	250	0	0	„
„ (maximum),	210	0	0	„	350	0	0	„

DETECTIVE DEPARTMENT.

	£	s.	d.		£	s.	d.	
2nd-rate Constable,	0	18	0	per week.	—			per week.
1st-rate „	1	0	0	„	—			„
Acting-Sergeant,	1	2	0	„	—			„
Full „	1	5	0	„	2	9	0	„
Acting-Inspector,	1	7	6	„	2	17	3	„
Full „	1	10	0	„	3	15	11	„
Inspector,	2	13	10	„	4	16	9	„
Superintendent,	210	0	0	per year.	350	0	0	per year.

LONDON METROPOLITAN POLICE.

EXTRACT from REPORT of the CHIEF COMMISSIONER of POLICE to the HOME SECRETARY, dated April, 1871.

PAY, CONDUCT, DRILL, and DISCIPLINE.

Careful consideration has been given to the important question of the rate of pay granted to the various ranks in the force, and several alterations and additions have been sanctioned by the Secretary of State which have tended very much to remove causes of dissatisfaction, and increase the efficiency and popularity of the service.

The rate of pay granted to the sergeants had long been considered too low; a constable on promotion to the rank of sergeant only receiving an addition of one shilling per week to his pay, while his duties and responsibilities were greatly increased, and there was no inducement, consequently, to men to qualify themselves for promotion.

An increase of three shillings per week has been granted to the sergeants, and of one shilling per week to the constables.

The inadequacy of the pay of the sergeants in charge of stations has also been recognised, and their position improved by an increased allowance of 4s per week.

A boon has been granted to the inspectors by the appointment of a chief inspector to each division, with an allowance of 1s. 6d. per diem.

The question of the salaries of the superintendents has also been considered, with the view of holding out inducement to those valuable officers to remain in the service, their salaries having been hitherto fixed with no annual increase for length of service. There are at present no less than 26 superintendents drawing pensions from the police fund.

It has been decided, that for the future, the salaries of the superintendents, instead of being as at present fixed at £300 per annum, shall commence at £250, and increase annually by £10, to a maximum of £350.

The rates of pay allowed to the members of the Metropolitan Police are given in return No. 22.

I think they are now, generally speaking, on a satisfactory footing, and on a scale fairly graduated to the duties and requirements of each rank. With the exception of the City Police, they are better paid than any constabulary in the kingdom.

The married men of the police, however, suffer in many divisions a great drawback from the difficulty and cost of obtaining suitable lodgings near their stations. I shall be glad when sufficient funds are available to provide quarters for more married men.

The re-organization of the reserves, and the increased allowances granted to them have been attended with good results. The reserves now form a special class, selected for ability, smartness, and good conduct, available in all special emergencies; and whereas formerly it was difficult to induce men to join the reserves, they are now an object of laudable ambition.

No. 22

WEEKLY RATES of PAY.

	£	s	d
Fourth class ordinary constable,	1	0	0
Third　　〃　　　〃	1	3	0
Second　〃　　　〃	1	4	0
Second　〃　reserve	1	6	0
First　ordinary　〃	1	6	0
First　reserve　〃	1	7	6
Divisional detective,	1	8	0
Second class ordinary sergeant,	1	9	0
First　　〃　　　〃	1	11	0
Second　〃　reserve	1	13	0
First　　〃　　　〃	1	14	0
Station, divisional, detective, and clerk sergeants,	1	13	0
Second class detective sergeants at chief office,	2	2	0
First　　〃	2	17	8
Second class ordinary inspector,	2	5	6
Second　〃　reserve	2	9	6
First　ordinary　〃	2	13	6
First　reserve　〃	2	16	6
Chief inspector,	3	3	0
Detective inspectors at chief office,	3	16	11
Chief detective inspectors,	4	16	2
Superintendent, first year,	4	16	3
〃　second year,	5	0	0
〃　third　〃	5	5	11
〃　fourth　〃	5	7	9
〃　fifth　〃	5	11	7
〃　sixth　〃	5	15	6
〃　seventh　〃	5	19	5
〃　eighth　〃	6	3	1
〃　ninth　〃	6	7	0
〃　tenth　〃	6	10	10
〃　eleventh　〃	6	14	8

The reserve force allowances are included above, but the four good service allowances of £25 per annum to superintendents are not included.

D.

MANCHESTER POLICE.

London Times, 30th November, 1871.

POLICE WAGES AT MANCHESTER.—A Manchester Watch Committee have had under their consideration the rate of wages paid to the police force of this city, and unanimously recommended to the Council an advance of pay to every grade in the force below the Chief Constable. At present the weekly wages paid to an ordinary constable on entering the force are 21s. After two months' service he is raised to 21s., and subsequently to 22s. 6d., which is the maximum amount, exclusive of additions he may obtain by merit. Under the revised scale it is recommended that the wages to begin with shall be 21s. per week, as at present, but raised to 22s. instead of 21s. at the end of two months, and at the end of the first year he is to receive 23s.; at the end of the second year 24s., and at the end of the third year 25s., which, if he remain in the force nine years more—twelve years in all—will be further advanced by 6d. per week every three years, making the maximum (without merit) 30s. 6d. The merit system is to remain in operation precisely as at present, so that this 24s. 6d. may by merit be brought up to 25s. per week, the highest sum an ordinary officer can attain to, as against 25s. at present. The advance is to be retrospective, so that if confirmed by the Council several men who have been in the force twelve years will at once be advanced to 30s. 6d. per week. The superior officers are to be dealt with in an equally liberal manner. We understand that no formal application has been made for an advance by the men, the audit sub-committee, together with the Chief Constable, having brought the question before the Watch Committee, who have unanimously adopted the suggestions made to them. Their recommendations, of course, will have to be formally approved by the Council.—*Manchester City News.*

E.

LIVERPOOL POLICE.

Liverpool Daily Mercury, July, 1871.

The force is at present 58 men under the strength, and during the past three months the average number short has been 53; and, owing to the want of selection, candidates have to be at times admitted into the force who are below the standard of height, and are not quite as intelligent or well-educated as is desirable. Of the 256 constables who joined in the year 1870, 44 resigned before they had been in the force six months, and 23 who had been less than twelve months, and 17 were allowed to resign from incapacity or misconduct under six months' service; a considerable loss was thus entailed upon the borough. The sub-committee are of opinion that it is essential that the strength of the force should be kept up, as the number of police constables is small in comparison with the population of the town, and the large extent and amount of valuable property to be protected in the docks and warehouses, and on the dock quays. It is also most important that its efficiency should be maintained by endeavouring to draw recruits from the more intelligent and better educated portion of the labouring classes, and by retaining in the force constables who have had one or more years' training and experience. To successfully achieve three objects, it is necessary that the rate of pay and conditions of service existing in the force should be such as will attract eligible recruits, and induce men to remain in the force when once they have entered. Your committee have caused inquiries to be addressed to the head-constables and watch committees of the large towns and more important counties. Replies have been received from Manchester, Lancaster, City of London, Leicester, Hull, Bristol, Bradford, Birmingham, Edinburgh, Glasgow, Leeds, Staffordshire, West Riding of Yorkshire, and the following is a resumé of them. A general difficulty appears to be experienced in keeping up the strength of the various forces, which is ascribed to the superior pecuniary inducements offered by other avocations. The rate of wages in the county of Lancaster, which more immediately comes into competition with our force, is as follows:—1st class constable, on appointment, 22s. 6d. per week; after three years' service, 23s. 11d.; after further service of four years, 24s. 6d. 2nd class constable, on appointment, 22s. 2d. per week; 3rd class constable, on appointment, 21s. 7d. Class of merit 1s. 2d. additional.*

The average rate of wages paid to constables of the lowest class, in the eight large English towns, is 19s. 10½d. per week, and of the 1st class constables, 23s. 6d. per week.

Your sub-committee submit that the rate of wages paid to constables, and the conditions of service are less favourable in the Liverpool police force than in the towns referred to, and in the county of Lancaster, and they believe that since the last revision in 1863 there has been a considerable increase in the cost of living and in rent in this town, and further, that the wage of unskilled labourers have advanced from 21s. to 24s. per week, and in consequence our police force has to compete on unfavourable terms for recruits, and fails to offer sufficiently strong inducements to men to remain in the force.

1. Your sub-committee are therefore of opinion that it is desirable, in order to keep up the efficiency of the force, to form a class to which constables who have seen long service, and have been exemplary in their conduct, and diligent in the discharge of their duties, but who are not qualified to act as bridewell-keepers or inspectors, can be promoted.

2. That the rate of pay of the 4th class be advanced 1s. per week, making it 21s. gross, or 20s. 2d. net.

3. That, with the exception of promotion to the merit class, and 1st class (which it is desirable to limit as to numbers), promotion shall be entirely by virtue of good conduct, efficiency, and length of service. The abolition of the limit as to numbers in the 2nd and 3rd class cannot fail to be a great incentive to good conduct and diligence, and an inducement to men to continue in the force.

4. That it is desirable to extend the leave with pay, as the time now allowed is not sufficient to enable the men to visit their friends.

The sub-committee would therefore recommend, that

1. A new class, to be called a merit class, be formed, limited to 20, in which the gross wages will be 26s. per week, and to which a constable will be only eligible for promotion as a reward for especial diligence and good conduct, and after a service in the force of not less than five years, and he must have been clear of reports for a space of three years.

2. That the number of 1st class constables be increased to 125, promotion to be dependent upon diligence, efficiency, and good conduct, and that a constable be eligible for promotion to this class after four years' service, and two years free from reports.

3. That the number of 2nd class constables be unlimited, and the rate of wages 23s. per week, and that a constable shall be eligible for promotion to this class for efficiency and good conduct after two years' service, and one year free from reports.

4. That the number of 3rd class constables shall be unlimited, and the rate of pay 22s. per week, and a constable shall be eligible for promotion to this class provided he is sufficiently efficient, has been six months in the force, and free from reports for a similar period.

5. That seven days' leave of absence, with pay, be given to the constables, and fourteen days to inspectors.

6. Your sub-committee believe that these modifications in the pay and conditions of service existing in the force, while entailing a comparatively small additional cost to the borough, will be greatly conducive to the general efficiency of the force.

(Signed),   W. B. FORWOOD, Chairman.

20th July, 1871.

STATEMENT SHOWING THE INCREASED COST WHICH WOULD BE INCURRED BY THE ADOPTION OF THE REPORT.

Present weekly rates of pay:—

	£	s.	d.
100 at 24s.	£120	0	0
200 „ 23s.	230	0	0
300 „ 21s.	310	0	0
180 „ 20s.	180	0	0
780	£840	0	0 × 52 = £43,680 0 0

Proposed weekly rates of pay:—

	£	s.	d.
20 at 26s.	£ 26	0	0
125 „ 24s.	150	0	0
333 „ 23s.	451	19	0
146 „ 22s.	160	12	0
96 „ 21s.	100	16	0
	£889	7	0 × 52 = £46,244 4 0

F.

Irish Times newspaper, January, 1872, alluding to police wages at Stafford and Chester.—

METROPOLITAN POLICE FORCE.

TO THE EDITOR OF THE IRISH TIMES.

Dublin, January 4th.

SIR,—For some time past I have been reading letters in your paper from telegraph clerks, banks, &c., &c., each advocating his own claim to an increase of salary. If you would have no objection, I would feel obliged by your insert-

ing a letter from one who is not a clerk, but a far worse treated individual—viz., a policeman. Our grievances are many, a few of which I will lay before your readers. We are on the streets for the protection of the life and property of the citizens of Dublin, or at least so it was intended; but unfortunately for us it is not the citizens lives that are in danger, but our own; for by a late order a constable is placed on every hospital in the city for the purpose of getting all vehicles disinfected that may arrive at the hospital with persons suffering from contagious or other diseases. To do this you meet as many as may seek vehicles to the Disinfecting Chamber in Marrowbone-lane, and see that everything in it is thoroughly disinfected. The constable is not disinfected, it being, I presume, immaterial whether he contracts disease or not. So well is this understood that he must enter houses where the believes small-pox patients are, and endeavour to get the friends of the person suffering to have him or her conveyed to hospital at once. Now, this duty is dangerous in the highest degree, yet it is done with reluctance, so as to rid and assist the sanitary authorities of the city in preventing the spread of a deadly disease. If any member of the force objects to this duty, he will be severely punished. If not engaged as above, he will be on regular street duty, and it is more than likely that before he is one hour out he will find it necessary to call a car to have himself conveyed to the nearest hospital to get wounds dressed which he has received in the execution of his duty as a peace officer. A policeman has to do this for the munificent sum of 13s., 16s. 2d., 17s. 6d., and 10s. per week—such being the weekly wages of the four rates; and to reach the two last mentioned sums you must serve six and eight years respectively. May we hope that the member for the University will, during the coming session, be good enough to include us in his list of underpaid "civil" servants; and further considering the great risks we are running for the well-being of his citizens, it is not, I think, too much to expect the city members to bring our case under notice, and the corporation to support it. Apologising for trespassing so much,—I remain, sir, your obedient servant,   ALPHA.

DUBLIN METROPOLITAN POLICE.

TO THE EDITOR OF THE IRISH TIMES.

SIR,—In your valuable Journal of this day I have seen a letter written on our service. In that letter the writer states the different rates in the gross without showing any stoppages. Now, for instance, take a man on third rate, that is, 16s. 6d., he has to pay barrack rent, 1s. 3d.; he also has many other deductions. Again, a man will serve 15 years and get a pension, but it will be only one in seven, for on the rate given above, 15 years will get 5s. per week to live on, and perhaps the man will have a wife and family to look to him. Trusting the authorities will take our case into consideration, with the rise of every article of provision,—I remain, sir, yours truly,   BETA.

THE DUBLIN METROPOLITAN POLICE.

TO THE EDITOR OF THE IRISH TIMES.

SIR,—In connexion with my former letter, which you were so kind as to insert, perhaps you would allow me to make some further remarks on the subject of an increase of salary to the Dublin police, to place before your readers what inducements there are to young men to remain in the force at present, and the counter-inducements held forth by the heads of different police forces in England. For a period of six years a constable here is living on a salary of from 15s. to 16s. 9d. per week, subject to deductions, which reduce it to 12s. or 14s. This is the amount paid to men of short service, and whom it is highly desirable should be made to consider the police as a good permanent situation for them. Apart from other causes their wages is not, I submit, sufficient to cause those remaining in the police longer than it suits their own convenience; neither is there any prospect for them in the future, for a full sergeant's pay is but 22s., and it is impossible at the present rate of promotion to reach that rank under 10 years' service. Allowing for your being a good character and an efficient constable; and as for retiring allowance, a constable joining now must serve 40 years for full pay pension. I am putting the case as plainly as I can, but certainly I am leaving out important deductions in the shape of sick pay, &c. I think, sir, you will agree with me, that a remuneration such as this is not sufficient, particularly when we find the chief constables of shires in England advertising in your paper for men to join their force, and giving a preference to members of the Dublin police. On comparing the salaries paid to the men of the different forces, it will be seen that the pay in England is in some cases double, but in all cases exceeds by one and a half the salary paid here. The chief of the Staffordshire police offers a salary

of 18s. per week, increased to 24s. after one year's service, with retiring allowance. At Chester, men were wanted at 24s. per week, but no retiring allowance; with as no constable joining now need ever expect to reach the service necessary to insure him a pension. In England a policeman does not suffer or undergo any of the dangers that men of the same profession encounter here. I have endeavoured to place before your readers a fair statement of facts, and by it will be seen how policemen are paid here and in England. In my former letter I appealed to the public on the ground of the essential services we are rendering to the citizens at present; but in this letter I briefly, but I am afraid feebly, endeavoured to point out to our own authorities and the Government the injurious comparison that exists in the payment of men performing duties alike, and situated so near each other. Under the present system of paying men, I can foresee a time when the Dublin police will be as a thing of the past,—I remain, sir, your obedient and much obliged servant,
ALPHA.

" A member of the Dublin Metropolitan Police" writes to us on the subject of an increase of pay to the force, which he regards as a matter of justice and right. The present scale of remuneration, he says, is wholly insufficient to provide the common necessaries of life. The pay of a third-class constable—and this class constitutes the majority of the force—is, it appears, only 16s. 9d. a week, but from this a deduction of 2s for barrack rent, &c, is made, leaving our civic guardians of this class in receipt of the magnificent weekly stipend of 14s. 9d—certainly not an extravagant sum. After six years' service a constable receives 17s. 6d., minus 2s. as before, and having served between eight and nine years he may be promoted to first-class, and receive 19s. per week. The superannuation arrangements are still more niggardly and objectionable; and our correspondent trusts that the Government will take the case of the Dublin Metropolitan Police into serious consideration during the ensuing session. Another member of the force complains of the long hours during which the men are on duty—a circumstance which must materially impair their physical strength, and retard their usefulness in seasons of emergency. In the different departments of the civil service, banks, &c., the hours of business vary from five to six and seven, with only part of Saturday. A policeman's hours of service in Dublin are—on day duty, nine and ten hours on alternate days for one month, and at night, eight and six and a half alternately for a similar period. Our correspondent says the force would be satisfied with a reduction of one hour each day and the same at night, which could, he thinks, be done without injury to the service, and he asks the Commissioners to bring the case of the men before the proper authorities.

G.

BOROUGH OF ASHTON-UNDER-LYNE POLICE FORCE
TO POLICE OFFICERS AND OTHERS.

Wanted, a smart active young man, not less than 5 feet 9 inches in height, for service in the above force.

Wages, on appointment, 23s. per week, with the chance of being raised for good conduct and efficiency, as follows, viz —2nd class, weekly, 24s ; 1st class, 25s. ; merit, 26s.

Each man is provided with a suit of good uniform clothing annually, he is also allowed eight days' leave of absence during summer months, and one day per month; total, twenty days annually, with full pay.

This offers an eligible opportunity to married men with families, inasmuch as plenty of work may be obtained in the neighbourhood for children at high wages.

Application, in applicant's own handwriting, accompanied with testimonials, to be sent to the Chief Constable, Town Hall, Ashton-under-Lyne.

GEORGE DALGLISH, Chief Constable.

Borough Police Station, Town Hall,
Ashton-under-Lyne.

COLONEL LAKE—

His Excellency presumes that the Dublin Metropolitan Police Force is not recruited exclusively from Dublin, and would feel obliged by being furnished with a statement showing the counties from which the Force has been recruited for the last five years.

Can a return be procured of the rate of wages of other classes in Dublin, besides the quay porters, and a comparison of the present rate of wages with that given when the present rate of pay of the Police was paid?

When was the present rate fixed?

What is the present system of recruiting?

T. H. B.

Metropolitan Police Office, Castle,
6th May, 1872.

In accordance with the minute of the Under Secretary on the accompanying file, the Commissioner of Police begs to submit the information required, viz. :—

1. A return showing the number of recruits who joined the force from each county in Ireland during each of the last five years, with an explanation of the present system of recruiting.

2. A comparative return showing the pay of the Metropolitan Police, and the rates of wages of other classes in Dublin besides quay porters before April, 1867, when the pay of the Police was raised, and at the present time.

The Commissioner trusts these returns will afford satisfactory information on the points referred to.

H. ATWELL LAKE.

The Under Secretary, &c.

RETURN showing the NUMBER of RECRUITS who joined the Dublin Metropolitan Police for the past five years, and the Counties they came from.

Counties.	1867.	1868.	1869.	1870.	1871.	Total.
Louth,	1	2	2	3	2	10
Meath,	13	14	17	15	8	69
Westmeath,	9	6	8	8	2	28
Dublin,	16	8	7	12	11	53
Kildare,	24	23	18	28	10	07
King's County,	5	3	10	4	4	23
Queen's County,	10	9	5	5	7	36
Carlow,	5	10	6	2	3	26
Wicklow,	30	19	25	37	19	130
Wexford,	6	3	9	10	10	34
Longford,	4	3	8	7	2	10
Kilkenny,	3	3	1	3		8
Londonderry,	2		2			4
Antrim,	3	1			1	2
Down,					1	1
Armagh,	6					6
Tyrone,	3	1	3	1		4
Monaghan,	1				1	2
Donegal,				1	1	2
Fermanagh,	3		3	3	3	9
Cavan,	1	1		3	2	20
Cork,	1		1	3		5
Clare,						
Limerick,	5	1		1		11
Tipperary,	1	1	1		8	13
Kerry,	1			1	3	5
Waterford,	3					3
Roscommon,				2		8
Sligo,	3	1	3	3	3	5
Galway,						
Mayo,			2	1	3	5
Leitrim,			2	1	3	5
Total,	158	117	124	182	109	634

REMARKS.

The system of recruiting is—when a candidate of the prescribed age and height presents himself for appointment, is on examination pronounced fit for the service by the medical officer, can at least read and write, is of an ordinary amount of intelligence, and bears a good character, on inquiry, as well as being recommended by a gentleman or respectable householder to whom he is known for the last five years at least ; he is then sent to the Depôt for training, if a vacancy exists there for him, and if there is no vacancy (as was the case generally till the last few years), he is directed to return home until written for when it becomes his turn to fill a vacated place in the Depôt.

A sufficient number of candidates—and generally more than needed to afford opportunity for selection—came forward until late years, at the inducement of friends serving in the force or those retired on pension ; but lately members in the service advise their young friends to the contrary when the former are joined long enough to experience the duties of the Police, and to discern the small pay they receive when compared with that obtained by similarly qualified persons without the restraint of discipline, or the danger and disrelish experienced in police duties.

[TABLE

TABLE showing a comparison between the Pay received by the Police and that received by other bodies in Dublin before April, 1867, and at present.

DUBLIN METROPOLITAN POLICE.

Ranks.	Yearly pay before revision in 1867.	Present pay yearly.	Yearly Increase.
	£ s. d.	£ s. d.	£ s. d.
Superintendents,	200 0 0	210 0 0	•
Inspectors, 1st Class,	121 1 0	123 0 0	1 19 0
Do. 2nd „	113 8 0	115 0 0	1 11 0
Do. 3rd „	105 17 0	107 0 0	1 3 0

* Before the revision the pay of Superintendents commenced at £180 yearly and went up by a yearly increment of £8 to £200, the maximum. At present the minimum is £198, which increases by £6 yearly to £213, the maximum.

Ranks.	Weekly pay before revision in 1867.	Present pay weekly.	Increase weekly.
	£ s. d.	£ s. d.	£ s. d.
Acting Inspectors,	1 6 0	1 6 0	—
Do.	1 5 8	1 6 0	0 0 4
Sergeants,	1 5 0	1 5 0	—
Do.	1 4 6	1 5 0	0 0 6
Acting Sergeants,	0 19 6	1 0 0	0 0 6
Do.	0 19 3	1 0 0	0 0 9
Constables, 1st Class,	0 18 9	0 19 0	0 0 3
Do. do.	0 18 6	0 19 0	0 0 6
Do. 2nd Class,	0 16 9	0 17 0	0 0 0
Do. 3rd „	0 15 0	0 16 0	0 1 9
Do. do.	0 11 6	0 13 6	0 4 0

REMARK.—It will be seen that members of the same position in the service drew different pays before the revision, but since that the pay is the same to all of the same rank. This variety, previous to 1867, was caused by a good-service pay being added to a man's ordinary pay when he arrived at certain periods of years of service, his conduct considered. By the revised scale which commenced 1st of April, 1867, this good-service pay was abolished, a few pence were added to the weekly pay of some, and in some instances (as will be seen with a few constables of the G Division) a reduction was made to equalise all pays of the same rank, and the three classes of constables were made into four rates, the junior rates receiving the most substantial increase.

G, OR DETECTIVE DIVISION.

Ranks.	Weekly Pay, before Revision in 1867	Present Pay, Weekly	Increase, Weekly
	£ s. d.	£ s. d.	£ s. d.
Superintendent,	•	—	—
Inspector,	•	—	—
Acting Inspector, (1)	1 8 3	1 8 0	0 0 1
Do. (1)	1 7 4	1 8 0	0 1 1
Do. (1)	1 6 10	1 8 0	0 1 8
Do. (10)	1 6 1	1 7 0	0 1 0
Sergeants,	Nil.†	1 5 0	—
Acting Sergeants,	1 1 10	1 3 0	0 0 2
Constables, (1)	1 1 1	1 0 0	—
Do. (1)	1 0 10	1 0 0	—
Do. (1)	0 19 11	1 0 0	0 0 1
Do. (5)	0 19 8	1 0 0	0 0 4
Do. (1)	0 17 11	1 0 0	0 2 1
Do. (1)	0 16 2	1 0 0	0 3 10
Do. (1)	0 16 2	0 18 0	0 1 10

* Yearly pay—Before revised it was £200; at present it is £210.
† Yearly pay—Not appointed in 1867; present pay, yearly, £188.
‡ Before 1867 there were no sergeants in the G Division.
§ Reduction.
‖ Reduction.

All the members of the G Division, being employed on detective duty, wear plain clothes, for the purchase of which no allowance is given them; and the price of such clothes, if deducted from each man's yearly pay, would leave it considerably less than the pay of a man on a similar rank in any other Division.

DUBLIN CITY FIRE BRIGADE.

Ranks.	Weekly Pay, before Revision in 1867	Present Pay, Weekly	Increase, Weekly
	£ s. d.	£ s. d.	£ s. d.
Superintendent,	†	—	—
Lieutenant or Inspector,	†	—	—
Sergeant,	0 17 0	1 7 6	0 10 6
Sub.,	0 15 0‡	0 18 0	0 3 0
Do.	0 15 0§	1 0 0	0 5 0

* Yearly pay in 1867, £300; present pay, £300 yearly, with house, allowances, and man servant.
† Not appointed in 1867; present yearly pay, £160, with £20 additional for supervision of horses.
‡ Allowed lodgings.
§ Without lodgings. All ranks are supplied with uniform clothing, including boots.

DUBLIN PORTS AND DOCK POLICE.

Ranks.	Weekly Pay, before Revision in 1867	Present Pay, Weekly	Increase, Weekly
		£ s. d.	
Sergeant,	Nil *	1 15 0	—
Men,	Nil.*	0 18 0	—

* Only a few years appointed. They have only street hours duty daily, have no night or Sunday duty, are allowed uniform, and are not subject or physique for Dublin Metropolitan Police duty.

STEAMPACKET COMPANIES.

Ranks.	Weekly Pay, before Revision in 1867	Present Pay, Weekly	Increase, Weekly
	£ s. d.	£ s. d.	£ s. d.
Porters,	0 13 0	1 7 0	0 9 0
Corn Porters,	1 0 0	3 0 0	1 0 0

Paid per sack carried, which in 1867 was 1d., but is now increased to 2d., and in many instances amounts to 4½ weekly.

Ranks.			
	£ s. d.	£ s. d.	£ s. d.
Coal Porters,	0 17 0	1 0 0	0 3 0
Coal Carters,	0 16 0	1 2 0	0 4 0

GAS COMPANIES' EMPLOYÉS.

Ranks.	£ s. d.	£ s. d.	£ s. d.
Smiths,	1 10 0	1 16 0	0 6 0
Carpenters,	1 10 0	1 16 0	0 6 0
Stokers,	1 10 0	1 13 0	0 3 0†
Coke Wheelers,	0 18 0	1 6 0	0 8 0
Coke Coolers and Fillers,	0 18 0	1 1 0	0 0 0
Firemen,	1 1 8	1 1 0	Nil.
Lamplighters,	0 15 0	0 19 0	0 4 6

'BUS OR TRAMWAY COMPANIES.

Ranks.	£ s. d.	£ s. d.	£ s. d.
Drivers,	1 0 0	1 5 0	0 5 0
Do.	0 15 0	1 5 0	0 10 0
Conductors,	0 18 0	1 1 0	0 3 0
Do.	0 13 0	1 1 0	0 0 0
Checkers,	Nil.	1 5 0	—
Stablemen,	0 12 0	0 18 8	0 6 8

TRADES.

Ranks.	£ s. d.	£ s. d.	£ s. d.
Carpenters,	1 8 0	1 12 0	0 4 0
Bricklayers,	1 8 0	1 12 0	0 4 0
Do. Labourers,	0 12 0	0 18 0	0 3 0

As a general rule it will be observed that the increase given to civilian employés in Dublin since 1867 counts as many shillings weekly as the increase given to the police counts pence.

MEMORANDUM.

Present current retail prices of the undermentioned articles of food of average quality in Dublin—

	s. d.
Bread per 4lb. loaf,	0 5½
Butter, per pound,	1 5
Beef,	3d. to 1 3
Mutton,	0 11
Pork,	0 8
Bacon,	0 10
Cheese,	1 0
Tea,	3 4
Coffee,	2 0
Sugar,	0 5
Potatoes, per stone,	0 11
Cabbages, each,	0 1

The current prices of the same articles of food in London may be put down at the same. Police constables in all large cities and towns of the United Kingdom consume good sound food, and do not require dainties. The average cost of the mess dinner in a police barrack in Dublin is from 4s. to 5s. 3d. per week, and by inquiry it appears the cost of same in London is from 5s. to 5s. 3d. per week.

The stoppages from constables in Dublin, in lieu of barrack rent, coal, and cook's wages, amount to about 2s. 1d. per week, and in London to 2s. 3d. per week.

Two pairs of boots in the year are supplied gratis to each constable in London, but in Dublin they have to purchase their own boots, at an average cost of 21s. per year.

Inspectors are supplied with their uniform at the expense of the establishment in London, but in Dublin they are obliged to purchase it out of their salaries.

GEORGE TALBOT, Assistant Commissioner.

Metropolitan Police Office, Castle,
28th May, 1872.

In continuation of his Report to Government on the subject of the pay of the Metropolitan Police, dated 30th March
last, the Commissioner has the honour to make the following
observations for submission to Government.

The discontent at the smallness of the pay of the Dublin
Police when compared to that enjoyed by other Police forces
in England, the Commissioner regrets to say, still continues,
and he much fears it may increase. Since the date of his report, just two months ago, no less than 24 men have tendered
their resignations, and have left the force, making the number
of vacancies at present 118—a very large per-centage on the
authorised strength.

Among those who have left the service many are of several
years' standing—men of irreproachable character and most
efficient constables, whose loss it will be difficult to replace.

On being questioned as to the cause of their resigning, the
answer of one and all is that they like the force, and would
only be too glad to remain in it, were it not that the pay
they receive is barely sufficient to secure the necessary food.

Though there may be a certain amount of exaggeration
in their assertion, there can be no doubt that at the present
prices of provisions the expense of living is very much
greater than it was a short time ago, and that it is quite
equal to what it is in England.

The Commissioner would refrain from so soon bringing
this subject again to the notice of Government, feeling well
assured that it has already engaged their attention; but the
urgency of the case must plead his excuse, as the demands

on the services of the Police are at this moment far greater
than can be met.

Deducting the number of men employed specially, there
are at present but 481 constables for duty, day and night—
namely, 243 by day and 238 by night, allowing, with the
relief, 123 patrols of the former, and 59 only of the latter,
in consequence of the beats being doubled at night.

Taking into consideration that the Police district extends
as far as Ballybrack in one direction, and that the important
town of Kingstown and other minor towns require a considerable number of Police for the due preservation of the
peace and the protection of property, the Commissioner
would not feel that he was justified in withholding from
Government the facts he has now ventured to lay before
them.

HENRY ATWELL LAKE.

The Under Secretary, &c.

FOR THE WHOLE DISTRICT.

Day, ...	241 constables }	482
Night, ...	241 " }	
1. Day Relief, . . .	120 " }	241
2. Day Relief, . . .	121 " }	
1. Night Relief, being doubled, .	120 "	—60 patrols.
2. Night Relief, being doubled, .	120 "	—60 patrols.

GEORGE TALBOT, Assistant Commissioner.

30th May, 1870.

30th May, 1872.

RETURN showing the Number of OFFICERS and CONSTABLES employed otherwise than on STREET DUTY.

How employed, &c.	Superintendents	Inspectors	Acting Inspectors	Sergeants	Acting Sergeants	Constables	
Commissioner's Office, .	.	.	.	.	2	3	
Chief Superintendent's Office, .	.	.	1	1	1		
Superintendents' Offices, .	.	.	1	9		6	
Magistrates' Offices, .	.	.	2	1	2	13	
In charge of Cells, .	.	.	.	.	.	31	
Reserves in Stations, .	.	.	.	.	.	31	For Police Vans.
Mounted Troop and Vans, .	.	1	.	1	1	27	
In charge of General Store, .	.	1	.	.	1	1	
Regimental Staff and Messmen, .	.	.	.	.	.	8	
Fixed and Stationary Beats, .	.	.	.	.	.	8	
Clothing and Bed, .	.	.	.	3	4	.	
Leave, .	.	2	.	3	3	10	
Leave, without Pay, .	.	.	.	.	.	2	
Suspended, .	.	.	.	.	.	2	
Drill, .	.	.	.	.	1	.	Hospitals, Banks, Botanic
Special Duty, .	.	.	.	.	3	55	Gardens, Dog Duty, Market
Sanitary Duty, .	.	.	.	1	3	8	Duty.
Sick, .	2	6	.	4	3	51	
Mission House, .	.	.	.	.	.	2	
Carriage Department, .	.	.	.	.	.	3	
General Post Office, .	.	.	.	.	.	2	
Hackney Carriage Inspection, .	.	.	5	1	.	10	
Duty at Rathmines, .	.	.	.	.	.	6	
Recruits on Reserve, .	.	.	.	.	.	8	
Not available for actual Street Duty, .	2	13	18	25	29	259	
Authorised strength, .	6	26	33	67	86	896	40 Supernumeraries.
Vacancies, .	.	.	.	.	.	86	33 "
Present strength, .	6	25	33	67	86	740	7 "
Not available for Street Duty, .	2	13	18	25	29	259	
Total for Street Duty, .	4	13	35	42	57	483	

RETURN, showing present authorised STRENGTH of the
G DIVISION, and how employed.

1 Superintendent.
1 Inspector.
13 Acting Inspectors.
4 Sergeants.
6 Acting Sergeants.
19 Constables.

NOTE.—One acting inspector and six constables are employed on carriage duty.

Five constables are employed from 8½ A.M. to 7 P.M. each
day, searching the pawn-offices for stolen and lost property,
as described to the Police.

One acting sergeant is employed as clerk in the Chief

Superintendent's Office, and one constable is employed as
clerk in the Detective Office, Exchange-court, keeping index
of reports received.

One acting inspector and one acting sergeant are employed at North-wall, watching arrivals from England, in
the way of concealed arms.

One constable is employed as reserve in Detective Office,
posting routes in the guard-books for reference; and the
Division is two short of its effective strength, owing to the
discharge from ill health of Entwisle and Mitchell.

DANIEL RYAN, Superintendent.

APPENDIX II.

MEMORIAL OF THE DUBLIN METROPOLITAN POLICE.

To the Chief Commissioner of the Dublin
Metropolitan Police.

This Memorial on behalf of the Officers and Constables of the Force is respectfully submitted, with the view of obtaining an adequate increase of pay, and other considerations, as may, upon investigation, appear reasonable and just to be granted to the several ranks and classes of the establishment.

Humbly Showeth,—

That since the formation of the present Police establishment in the Dublin Metropolitan District, now nearly thirty-five years ago, the force has been directed with such uniformity of discipline, and attention to the requirements of the public, that security to the person and safety to the property of the citizen, preservation of the peace, and general good order, have been maintained by the force alone, without aid from any other quarter, though at times great political excitement frequently disturbed the metropolitan district, and caused heavy labour and extraordinary vigilance upon the part of the Police, which officers and constables cheerfully met, through much opposition, and frequently with considerable danger to themselves. The steady bearing and good conduct of the force on such occasions merited and received the approbation of the Government and the public at large. The gracious thanks of members of the Royal Family who have visited Dublin, and observed the perfect arrangements made by the Police in the city, have been conveyed to the force, from time to time, by the Commissioners, and highly appreciated by the men. The several Lords Lieutenant, nearly all the Judges, and the Magistrates, have expressed satisfaction with the manner in which the Dublin Metropolitan Police have discharged their public duties during the most trying times. Thus, whilst the services rendered by the Police have been gratefully acknowledged and favourably commented upon, the remuneration or pay of the men of this service is less than that of any other similar Police force, and considerably under that of the London Police, which it most resembles in constitution; and whilst the wages of the artisan and all the working classes have been considerably advanced for some time, and is still increasing—in many cases from 50 to 100 per cent.—with the requirements of the times and the increased cost of living, and the working man's hours of labour lessened, the pay and duties of the Dublin Police force remain unaltered; and as the pay now stands, it is almost impossible for the man to procure all the necessaries required for the position the policeman has been hitherto supposed to fill—viz., that of being independent and free of debt. The attached Abstract (A) has been carefully compiled to show the expenses which are unavoidable, and must in some way be met and discharged by the constable, who, if a married man, with a family to support, must live on inferior food, and be always in very straitened circumstances, indeed.

That from the severe nature of the Police duties, the smallness of the pay, and amount of stoppages from that sum, as well as the discouragement to long service by the present Superannuation Act (30 & 31 Vic., cap. 95), many of the most active, intelligent, and promising young men have resigned the service, leaving an unusual number of vacancies, for some time past, in the force. The heavy nature of the duties of the Dublin Police are clearly ascertained by comparing them with those of the London Police, and from the published statistics of both services. One sufficient fact will show that during the past two years the number of prisoners arrested by both services were—By the London Police, which numbers something over 9,100 men, 145,230; and by the Dublin Police, consisting of 1,060, of all ranks, 62,397. In this duty of arresting prisoners—a work which necessitates much subsequent trouble, loss of rest and sleep to night-duty constables, the Dublin Police performed nearly four times as much duty as the London force. In other matters of duty the statistics will show a very favourable contrast on the part of the Dublin Police, whose willing obedience to legal commands, coolness, and perseverance evinced by the men when carrying out the orders of superiors to suppress riot and disorderly conduct in the city, greatly increased the severity of their ordinary duties during the year ended 1871. Many officers and constables suffered severely from injuries inflicted in discharge of important duties during that year. There were so many as 175 persons made amenable to the law for having assaulted and obstructed the Police, and for attempting to rescue prisoners. In addition to this great opposition by evil-disposed persons to the peace

officer, there have been 226 cases of more or less grievous assaults committed on the men, in which the offenders were not made amenable. No less than 213 members of the force were compelled, from severe injuries, to place themselves under the care of the medical officers during the past year; some of these men were permanently disabled from the effects of injuries alone.

That considering the very severe nature of the duties—the length of time men are employed during the seven days of the week—Sunday only occasionally excepted—averages fifty hours at night, and sixty hours, at the least calculation, by day—during the week, besides those extra hours, not easily estimated, which all active members of the force spend at Police courts, coroners' inquests, and other public business, all go to prove that the utility and efficiency of the Dublin Police is unsurpassed by any other similar force in the Empire, whilst no other "Civil Service" can approach it, as regards the terrible severity of its duties, and the amount of work performed, yet it is the worst and most inadequately paid service in the empire. Memorialists viewing the position, and carefully comparing the situation of the police service with that of other public departments, confidently expect that their case will receive due and favourable attention, and that the following requests may be considered reasonable:—

First.—That an adequate increase be granted to the pay of all constables, acting sergeants, sergeants, and acting inspectors, to raise such pay on an equality with that of the London Metropolitan Police, and that no deductions in future be made on account of lodging or fuel, from their pay—that an allowance of coal or other fuel be granted, or an equivalent in money, paid weekly, to all married men of these ranks who are not provided with quarters by the service, and that proper regulation boots and gloves, to be worn while on duty, be supplied at the public expense; and that the expense of properly fitting uniform clothing hitherto paid by the men, shall in future be otherwise discharged, or a sufficient allowance granted to each man for that purpose; and that in the event of sickness arising from performance of duty, no deduction be made from the pay of any member of the force while on the sick list, except under circumstances where the medical officers shall consider it necessary to recommend some deduction to be made.

The men of the unmarried branch of the service desire to bring under the notice of the Chief Commissioner the expenses they invariably incur for the purchase of gloves suited for the troop, above a superior class of boots, and the constant wear and tear of shining and other clothing, from hard work in the stable and while on duty. These men request that while they belong to the unmarried police a sufficient allowance may be added to their pay to cover all necessary outlay.

The officers and men of the detective division are deserving of special consideration as regards their peculiar position in the force. Each of these men has been selected from amongst the well-trained and exceptionally well-conducted constables of other divisions for some special qualification required in a detective officer, and they have been found expert in bringing most of the old habitual thieves in the city to justice, and instrumental in recovering for the owners stolen goods and valuables to large amounts. These officers possess considerable knowledge of police duties, great intelligence, patience, and perseverance, as have been proved by their acts when tested before magistrates, crown solicitors, judges, and juries in Dublin and elsewhere; in all important cases they seldom fail in receiving special commendation for zeal, ability, impartial and truthful evidence given on oath.

The detective branch has been found not only equal to its work in the pursuit of skilled thieves located in Dublin, or those of the swell mob who visit occasionally, but it has rendered valuable services to the State in bringing under the notice of the authorities the movements of political conspirators, and making the most dangerous of them amenable to justice, as well as frustrating their plans and rendering their movements, leading to evil purposes, harmless, since the beginning of the "Young Ireland" conspiracy in 1848 to the Fenian movement of recent times. The meritorious and valuable services of the officers and men of the detective branch have been from time to time rewarded, but the standing very limited rates of pay of these officers have not been increased, and it is at present wholly insufficient for their wants. In nearly all cases of importance, private expense, to attain success in pursuit of an object sought, has to be incurred by nearly all the officers, and these items cannot be afterwards recovered. The detective officers must always appear respectably dressed, and fit to enter any company where their appearance and dress should not be that of a policeman, and to keep up the position requires considerable private outlay. The officers and men of this branch of the public service have been well tried in every way, found so useful by the Government, and the commercial public, that it is but just to place them on a par with the London detective police, by granting them similar rates of pay, and equal rank as detectives.

The inspector of police, the chief station-house officer in a sub-division, whose hours of duty, indoor and outdoor, in all weathers, half by day and half by night, count during the week nearly eighty hours, may be considered the hardest worked officer in the service. The acting inspector, or second station-house officer, is likewise employed on duty the same length of time. These officers are well deserving of a substantial increase to their present very inadequate rates of pay as compared with the London officers of the same rank. The inspectors have, up to the present moment, to purchase, at considerable expense to themselves, their uniform clothing for the use of public service; these officers now respectfully request that in future all such uniform and necessary equipments to be used by officers of their position be supplied to them at the public expense.

The divisional superintendents, each of whom has charge of a district the population of which amounts on an average to about 60,000 people, is responsible to the Commissioners for the peace, good order, and security to life and property therein, as well as for the discipline, good conduct, and efficiency of all the officers and constables intrusted to his charge; for the care and cleanliness of barracks, station-houses, cells, all furniture, bedding and other public property on police premises, the payment of the men of his division, and all contingent expenses. The time occupied by each officer of this class varies from ten to fourteen hours day and night, Sunday included, in the performance of his various duties. The superintendents have to purchase their own uniform at considerable expense to themselves, and now beg respectfully to be granted a fair allowance for a respectable outfit in future, or that such may be supplied to them at the public expense; and they also request that the present limited allowances granted for rents of offices and other purposes be increased to a reasonable amount, and that the pay may be advanced and made equal to that of the officers of the same rank in the London Metropolitan Police.

The chief superintendent, being the next officer under the Commissioners, is accountable to them for the prompt execution of all orders within the Metropolitan Police District, and in the absence of the Commissioners he receives all telegrams and communications of importance requiring immediate attention, and he is the responsible police officer on such occasions; he is also accountable for the correctness of the Register (book) of the force, and these books containing the promotions, changes, and appointments in proper order of seniority, and all records and statistics of the service; the careful checking of estimates of pay for the accountant, the preparation of all general returns and reports required by the Government in times of elections, public meetings, processions, and excitement he has carried out the general police arrangements ordered by the Commissioners in the most satisfactory manner.

Memorialists now respectfully submit their claims for substantial increase of pay, and the redress of any matters requiring amendment or change, to the favourable consideration and best attention of the Chief Commissioner, and that such increase may date from the 1st of April in the present year, and Memorialists will ever pray.

ABSTRACT A REFERRED TO IN MEMORIAL.*

The following account of expenses necessary for the maintenance of a Dublin Metropolitan Police Constable on active duty is given on a calculation of present prices of provisions, &c. :—

Items, viz., Food, Lodgings, Necessaries.	Weekly Expenditure			Annual Expenditure		
	£	s.	d.	£	s.	d.
Average cost of breakfast weekly,	0	4	4	11	5	4
„ dinner „	0	8	2	21	4	8
„ supper „	0	4	4	11	5	4
Deduction from pay for lodging and fuel,	0	1	3	3	5	0
Payment to cooks, housemaid, and messenger,	0	0	11	2	7	8
Washing of shirts, sheets, stockings, &c.,	0	1	0	2	12	0
Tobacco, pipes, and matches,	0	0	4	0	19	6
Soap, blacking, candles, and cleaning stuff,	0	0	3	0	15	0
Two pair of boots annually,	—			1	12	0
Repairing same,	—			0	12	6
Three calico shirts, 12s., and six pairs of socks, 7s 6d.,	—			1	2	6
Two woollen shirts, 18s., and two pairs of drawers, 10s.,	—			1	2	0
Three pocket-handkerchiefs, 8s., and two towels, 2s.,	—			0	6	0
Four pairs of white gloves and two pairs of black,	—			0	6	6
Average annual cost of "plain clothes,"	—			2	10	0
Purchase of a watch after first year,	—			4	10	0
Repair and cleaning same,	—			0	2	6
Average cost of fitting uniform clothing,	—			0	7	6
Brushes, cooking utensils, knives, forks, and spoons,	—			0	5	0
Deduction from pay during sickness, &c.,	—			0	15	0
"Duty book," memo. book, paper, pens, and ink,	—			0	10	6
Total expenditure for men living in barracks,	—			67	13	3
Married men, { Rent of lodging,	0	4	6	11	14	0
{ Cost of fuel,	0	3	9	9	18	0
Expenses of a family consisting of eight persons, viz., two adults and six children. Breakfast, 1s. 3½d. per day,	0	9	3½	—		
Dinner, consisting of herrings and potatoes (butcher's meat once a day), 1s. 6d.,	0	9	11	—		
Supper, 1s. 3½d. per day,	0	9	7½	—		
Men in the "Troop" have to provide spurs and spur-boxes,	0	8	6			
And two pairs of leather gloves,	0	11	0			
	£0	19	6			

* I object to this Abstract as being, in my opinion, an exaggerated account in many of the items. H. ATWELL LAKE.

22nd October, 1872.

Return showing the Authorized Strength of Constables for each Division, the Number of Vacancies, the Number Specially Employed, and the Number Available for the Beat in each Division.

Division.	Authorized Strength	Vacancies	Specially employed.		Available for Beat duty.	Remarks.
			Paid for.	Not paid for.		
A, . .	138	14	4	15	105	The Constables of the Troop are included.
B, . .	152	19	8	12	104	
C, . .	155	17	10	15	113	
D, . .	155	24	9	15	106	
E, . .	114	22	—	11	81	
F, . .	112	18	—	—	88	
G, . .	19	—	—	—	19	
Total,	845	114	31	68	617	

H

The 31 men are paid for by the undermentioned establishments:—

	Men.	Total amount per annum.
		£. s. d.
Exhibition Building,	16	792 19 0
Four Courts,	5	247 18 9
Public Health Committee,	3	148 12 3
National Board of Education,	3	146 13 3
General Post Office,	2	90 1 0
Bank of Ireland,	1	49 10 0
East-street, North,	1	43 13 5
Total,	31	£1,529 15 11

The 53 men not paid for are employed as under:—

Commissioners' Orders and Store,	4
Superintendents' Office,	6
Magistrates' Officers,	14
Gaolers and Barrack Reserve,	33
Messmen, 9, at Mansion House, 2,	11
Sanitary Duty,	8
Veterinary Department,	3
Dog Duty,	1
Botanic Gardens, 1; and Jervis-street Hospital,	2
Total,	53

APPENDIX IV.

MEMORIALS SUBMITTED TO THE COMMISSION BY COLONEL LAKE.

A.—MEMORIAL of ASSISTANT COMMISSIONER.

Metropolitan Police Office, Castle,
October, 1872.

The Assistant Commissioner begs to draw the attention of the Chief Commissioner to the inadequate amount of his salary under the following circumstances:—

The Act of 22nd and 23rd Vic., cap. 52, passed in 1859, thirteen years ago, fixes the salary of Assistant Commissioner at £600 per annum (with an allowance of £40 a year for the keep of a horse), and appears to have been adopted upon the principle that at that time the salary of the Divisional Magistrates of Police was £600 per annum; now the salary of the Magistrates is £800, and the Chief Magistrate receives £960. The Assistant Commissioner is, like the magistrates, a justice of the peace for the counties of Dublin, Kildare, Wicklow and Meath. His duties are of the most varied and important nature ordinarily, and in the absence of the Chief Commissioner he exercises all his functions. A Divisional Magistrate, without any previous public service, on appointment, at once receives £800 a year. The Act evidently contemplated that the salary of the Assistant Commissioner and that of the Magistrates should be the same.

The Assistant Commissioner has now been in the public service above thirty-two years—nineteen years as Stipendiary Magistrate, and twelve years in the army. The Assistant Commissioners of the London Metropolitan Police receive salaries of £800 each, with allowances—for rent of £300, and for travelling expenses £150, making their total income £1,250 per annum. Even the District Superintendents of that force receive salaries, three at £630 and one at £750.

The Assistant Commissioner begs to draw the attention of the Commission to the increased cost of living since 1859 (including house rent, fuel, &c.), when the Act referred to was passed; to the fact that his pay is considerably less than that of the District Superintendent in London, and £200 less than that of the Junior Divisional Magistrate; that the forage allowance he receives, viz. £40, is wholly inadequate, as he is not allowed either a servant or allowance for one to groom his horse.

The Assistant Commissioner, however, will be perfectly satisfied with whatever may be the opinion of the Commission. If they think it right to recommend that any increase be given him, he will feel grateful, whether it be by increase of salary or allowance.

GEORGE TALBOT.

B.—MEMORIAL from the SECOND CLASS CLERKS soliciting INCREASE of SALARIES.

Metropolitan Police Office,
Castle, 24th October, 1872.

SIR,—We, the undersigned clerks of the 2nd class of your department, beg most respectfully to ask you to recommend to the Commission now sitting, that we be placed on a more liberal scale of salaries than we at present enjoy.

We need not refer to the cost of living, which you well know is very high, scarcely enabling us to live even a little more respectably than a mechanic; but as you are pleased to recommend the London scale of pay for your men, we would ask you to recommend us for an improved scale of salaries.

We therefore respectfully but earnestly request you will be pleased to forward this memorial to the Commission of Inquiry, and should further information be required on the subject, any one of us will be prepared to give it.

We have the honour to be, sir,

Your most obedient servants,

FRANCIS MOLTON,
WILLIAM PERRY,
ALFRED O'CONNOR,
G. O'HARLOW,
E. J. RYAN.

The Chief Commissioner,
Dublin Metropolitan Police.

C.—MEMORIAL from Dr. LONG, Apothecary to the Force, soliciting INCREASE of SALARY.

To HENRY ATWELL LAKE, Esq., C.B. A.D.C. to the Queen,
Chief Commissioner of the Police.

The MEMORIAL of P. W. LONG, M.D., L.R.C.S.I., Apothecary to the Dublin Metropolitan Police.

RESPECTFULLY SHOWETH—

That memorialist is in the sixteenth year of his service in the Medical Department of the police; that he is obliged to attend daily at the Castle for the performance of his duties.

That his salary of £30 per annum is an extremely small one for the responsible nature of the duties to be performed, and respectfully solicits an increase of pay commensurate with the vastly increased cost of living.

That from the time of his appointment in 1857 to the present, memorialist, in addition to his own special duties,

invariably assisted the head of his department in the medical treatment of the members of the force.

That memorialist has repeatedly been in sole medical charge of the force in the absence on leave of Dr. Ireland or Dr. Nedley, and that you were pleased to express your satisfaction at the manner memorialist performed such duty.

That memorialist earnestly requests the Chief Commissioner will kindly place this memorial before the Commissioners at present in Dublin for inquiring into the Civil Service, for their favourable consideration.

Memorialist, anxiously hoping that the Chief Commissioner will support its prayer, for which he shall feel ever grateful.

118, Stephen's-green, West,
23rd October, 1872.

APPENDIX V.

MEMORANDUM as to RELIEVING the REGISTRAR of CABS from all PECUNIARY RESPONSIBILITY.

It will be quite practicable to have the duties on hackney carriages lodged in bank by the licensees, in the same way as is done by pawnbrokers, whose licence duty (£100 Irish annually) forms part, like the carriage duties, of the revenues of the police establishment. No sum, for hackney carriage duty, will, as a rule, be less than £1.

With respect to the renewal licences of hackney-carriage drivers, issued annually, and the duty on each of which is 1s., the Commissioner of Police is of opinion that stamps, similar to those used in petty sessions proceedings and for dog licences, should be adopted. The renewal licences would be made out in the carriage office, as at present; they would then be sent, according to the addresses of the drivers, to the several police stations, and handed from the latter, where the driver would pay the 1s., and where the stamp would be affixed. This is the system at present in regard to pedlars' licences, and would effect a great improvement in the delivery of the drivers' licences, as the overcrowding of the carriage office and confusion which now exist would be entirely obviated—the licences being issued from sixteen police stations instead of from one office. Stamps would also be used in the case of new licences for conductors and drivers, 2s. 6d. fee. The superintendents of police would be supplied with books of such stamps, and would account for same weekly.

While upon this subject, the Commissioner of Police would suggest that monthly pensions should, like the quarterly pensions, be paid by cheque; no sum of £1 and upwards to be paid otherwise. This would reduce cash payments in the Accountant's office to very few and trifling disbursements, and would be a very desirable arrangement. The bank allows no interest on the police moneys.

The Commissioner of Police is quite of opinion that the bank should be utilised as much as possible, and that the more direct the payments into the bank are, without passing unnecessarily through several hands, the better.

Under the arrangement indicated in this memorandum, it will be quite feasible to carry out the views of the Commission, and not render it necessary to have any money received at the carriage registry office. The Commissioner will arrange the necessary details, including the receipt of the 10s., for the paid annually by publicans, on their licences, to the police. This latter can also be paid into the bank by the publicans themselves.

Respectfully submitted,

HENRY ATWELL LAKE,
The Commissioner of Police.

Metropolitan Police Office,
Castle, 11th November, 1872.

APPENDIX VI.

AUTHORIZED STRENGTH of the DUBLIN METROPOLITAN POLICE when the FORCE was ORIGINALLY ORGANIZED and NOW—NUMBER of RECRUITS and REMOVALS from the FORCE for the YEAR ended 1st OCTOBER, 1872.

This force was originally organized in 1837. At the commencement of 1838, when its duties in the streets first began, it consisted of 911 officers and men, but some additions being made to its strength in the course of that year, at its close the establishment consisted of 993 men.

In 1840, on a considerable extension of the police district into the suburbs, another augmentation of the force necessarily took place; so that, with some other subsequent trifling changes, the authorized strength of the establishment at the present time is 1,096.

ORIGINAL AUTHORIZED STRENGTH of the FORCE in 1837, and PRESENT AUTHORIZED STRENGTH.

YEARS.	Total Authorised Strength.	Superintendents.	Inspectors.	Acting Inspectors.	Sergeants.	Acting Sergeants.	Constables.
1837, At the present time (1873),	911	6	18	..	54	..	833
	1,096	70	26	..	60	72	63	846

The Act of Parliament establishing the force did not prescribe the numbers, but they were fixed, and the subsequent augmentations made by authority of the Treasury.

In 1838, twenty supernumeraries, for the first time, were added to the service, but they are not included in the authorized strength of the force.

In 1866, in order to meet the pressure caused by Fenianism and other pressing emergencies, the number of supernumeraries was authorized by Government to be continued at forty, to which number it had been increased, by due authority, in 1865, for the purpose of providing special police for the Dublin International Exhibition of that year.

This increase, however, is to be regarded as a temporary measure, and should twenty be found sufficient for the recruitment of the force, when the present vacancies therein have been filled up, the original number will be returned to.

The number of recruits available from 1st October, 1871, to the same date in 1872, was eighty.

The removals from the force in the same year were as follow, viz:—

† Voluntary resignations, ... 82
Dismissals, ... 43
Ill health, ... 46
Deaths, ... 17

Total, 188

There are now 114 vacancies.

H. ATWELL LAKE,
The Commissioner of Police.

Metropolitan Police Office,
Dublin Castle.

* Including one Chief Superintendent, authorized by Treasury in 1840.
† The number of voluntary resignations for the year is made up thus; seventy-two from January to September inclusive, as stated in the Commissioners' evidence, in reply to question No. 62, and ten during the months of October, November, and December, 1871.

TABLE showing the STRENGTH, PAY, and COST of LIVING of the following Police Forces:—LONDON METROPOLITAN,
number of the DAILY SICK, the VACANCIES, in September, 1872,

LOCAL FORCE	Pay of Superintendents	Pay of Inspectors	Pay of Acting Inspectors	Pay of Sergeants	Pay of Acting Sergeants	Pay of Constables
September, 1872. **LONDON MET. POLICE.** Strength, 9,948 Vacancies, 290 Daily sick, 3 per cent	From £4 7s. 2d. to £5 14s. 4d. per week (£241 or £4 to £250 3s. 3d. per annum), not including four "Good Service" allowances of £25 each	From £3 3s. 0d. to £4 16s. 2d. per week	None.	From £1 4s. to £2 15s. 6d. per week—this last being for Detectives	None.	From £1 to £1 8s. per week—this latter scale for Detective Division
CITY OF LONDON. Strength, 704 Vacancies, None Sick, daily, 1½ per cent.	Chief, £400 per ann Supt £300 do	From 40s. to 50s. per week	None	From 34s. to 40s. per week	Near	3rd class, No 90, 24s. per week 2nd " " 168, 28s do 1st " " 346, 30s. do The Constable generally arrives at 1st class in two years
LIVERPOOL. Strength, 1,207 Vacancies, 64 Sick, daily average, 3¾ per cent.	From £166 per annum to £275 do.	From 32s per week to £160 per ann; or £3 17s. 2d a week (nearly)	None	None.	None.	6th class, No 235, 22s. a week 5th " " 154, 23s. a week after 6 months' service 4th " No 44, 21s a week after 2 years' do 3rd " No 152, 24s a week after 3 years' do 2nd " No 94, 26s. a week after 6 years' do 1st " No 328, 27s a week after 8 years' do Detectives, from 28s to 34s. per week
GLASGOW. Strength, 807 Vacancies, — Sick, daily, 7 per cent.	£100 to £200 per annum	Lieutenants, £250 to £150, Inspectors, 30s. to 35s a week	None	22s to 30s.	None.	No. 128, 20s. per week " 107, 22s do " 272, 24s. do " 63, 26s. do Infants, 19s to 32s per week
MANCHESTER. Strength, 735 Vacancies, 51 Sick, daily, per cent.	£200 to £240 per annum	40s to 44s per week	None.	31s. to 35s per week	None.	22s. to 29s. per week, with additional pay for length of service. Merit class has £1 1s. 6d after 2 years' service, £1 8s after 6 years, and £1 to after 12 years. "Merit" class obtained irrespective of length of service
BIRMINGHAM. Strength, 400 Vacancies, 15	£100 per annum	45s 14s per week	None.	28s to 32s per week	None.	21s. to 24s a week. Merit class, 26s.
EDINBURGH. Strength, 543 Vacancies, 5	Lieutenants, £220 to £175 per ann.†	£110 to £100 per ann. (each 2s 6d to £2 1s deduction) per week.	None.	£2 7s. with 10 per cent	None.	1st year, 21s. a week 2nd " 22s. do 3rd " 23s. do
DUBLIN. Strength, 1,116 Vacancies, 124 Daily sick, 4 per cent	From £160 per ann to £264 16s independent of allowances for forage, groom, and rent of official residence.	From £315 per ann to £191 do; one Detective Inspector £182, including lodging allowances.	From £1 6s to £1 5s. 0d per week; he has to do same duty as Inspector, and arrives at the rank after about 17 years' service	£1 1s a week; arrives at this rank after about 14 or 15 years' service	£1; has the same duty as Sergeant; arrives at the rank about 11th year of service	4th class, 15s 6d. per week 3rd " 15s 6d afterwards do service 2nd " 17s 6d after 5 or 6 years' do 1st " 19s after 8 or 9 years' do Detectives, from 16s. to £1 a week

† These scales of pay have been raised since the Return was originally prepared.
‡ These scales of pay were raised 10 per cent. in the early part of this year.

DIX VII.

LONDON CITY, DUBLIN, LIVERPOOL, GLASGOW, MANCHESTER, BIRMINGHAM, and EDINBURGH; likewise the relative
the HEIGHT and AGE, ALLOWANCES, &c., &c.

Height and Age	Cost of Lodging	Cost of Living	Allowances.	Remarks
Height, 5 ft 6½ in Age, under 30 years	There are select houses in blocks attached to some of the station-houses, for married Sergeants, containing sculleries, lava-tories, and lavatories; the rent of three rooms, 3s 6d a week (3 this is the scale at the Southwark station.) The average rent paid by members of the force who live in lodgings is 4s. 6d. a week for two rooms.	Mess only at dinner. Cost of dinner and all barrack expenses, 5s a week, with breakfast and supper, about 9s. 6d. a week.	Two pairs of boots a year, men living out of stations are allowed 6d. a week for coals. Superintendent and Inspector allowed uniform or £11 or £10 each class in lieu thereof	The barracks contain handsome libraries, billiard-rooms, presses, each mess having two compartments for clothes and food; warm baths always ready; bands of music—stringed, reed, and brass; give classes and educational classes
—	Houses are prepared for married men, who are charged only a small rent, 1s 6d a week is charged for all barrack expenses.	About same as in London Metropolitan Police.	Boots.	A special feature of this Force is its hospital—a model institution of the kind—to which is mainly owing the exceptionally low "Daily Sick" rate. Every man unfit for duty from illness is treated here—shamming or malingering is consequently almost impossible. Superannuation fund is defrayed by the Town Council.
5 feet 8 inches; often lower.	6s. a week for two rooms	10s a week in barracks.	2s. a week for clothes, when uniform is not worn, many officers have free stationery and gas, and the higher officers are allowed for boots and bats. Uniform for all ranks.	A very good band, and an extremely efficient fire brigade, many men are in the force who resigned own.
—	Cost of lodging, from 6s. to 10s. 10d. a month, for two rooms	4s to 8s. 6d. a week in barracks, this includes breakfast, with ham and eggs, bread, butter, and tea, dinner, with ½ lb of cooked meat, soup, and vegetables, and supper, likewise all barrack expenses	Clothing and boots for officers and men; money for clothes to officers who wear no uniform.	Barracks and section-rooms spacious and well-exercised; very handsome offices for superintendents and Inspectors; dinners economy fair-rate, men are allowed to take gratuities for certain services not official.
5 feet 8 inches From 23 to 39 years of age.	Good board, lodging, and washing may be had outside barracks at 4s a week; 4s a week procures a house with four rooms.	Complete board and lodging, with all barrack expenses, 10s. 6d. a week.	Boots.	Statistical returns, complete and valuable; a very spacious parade room. On each story of barracks, baths, closet, and lavatory; walls painted in oil; and all the appointments neat and comfortable.
3 feet 7 inches. 22 to 34 years of age.	Two rooms, 2s 6d. to 3s 6d.; four rooms, 4s. 6d.	Breakfast and dinner and all servants' fees cost 11s. a week in barracks, good board and lodging outside, 12s a week.	Officers' uniform. Boots.	This force has no annual report—no printed tables or returns; has a band of music; baths in barracks, which are very neat and comfortable.
5 feet 7 inches. Age, 21 to 30.	Varies very much; some of the men live in very poor and mean lodgings.	No barracks; cost of living about 11s. per week.	6d. a week for boots.	—
5 feet 5 inches. 18 to 46 years of age.	4s. a week for two rooms.	In barracks—for dinner and barrack expenses alone, without breakfast or supper, 3s. 6d. per week.	There is no allowance, except uniform, to men under the rank of Inspector; nothing for boots, gloves, or coals; Superintendents and Inspectors have to purchase their own uniforms.	There are no baths; no water-closets, no presses for clothes; no annex, except hand bath; no sheets; no bands of music; no allowance for coal or boots; no allowance for uniform for the superior officers.

THOMAS NEDLEY, M.D., &c.,
Medical Officer of Dublin Metropolitan Police.

APPENDIX VIII.

INCREASED RATES of PAY given to the LONDON METROPOLITAN POLICE in NOVEMBER, 1872, and CONDITIONS upon which each CONSTABLE is admitted to the FORCE.

Whitehall, 27th November, 1872.

SIR,—In accordance with the request conveyed in your letter of the 4th instant, I am directed by Mr. Secretary Bruce to transmit for the information of the Irish Civil Service Enquiry Commissioners, the enclosed memoranda on the subject of the increased rate of pay of the Metropolitan Police Force, which have been furnished by the Commissioner of Police.

I am, Sir, your obedient servant,

A. F. O. LIDDELL.

The Secretary to the Irish Civil
Service Commissioners, 46, Upper
Sackville-street, Dublin.

ENCLOSURE A.

METROPOLITAN POLICE - RATES OF PAY.

CLASS AND RANK.	Rates of Weekly Pay, up to 11th Nov., 1872.			Present Rates of Weekly Pay.		
	£.	s.	d.	£.	s.	d.
4th Class Ordinary Constables,	1	0	6	1	4	0
3rd " " "	1	3	0			
2nd " " "	1	6	0	1	7	0
2nd " Reserve "	1	8	0	1	10	0
1st " Ordinary "	1	7	0	1	11	0
1st " Reserve "	1	9	0	1	13	0
Divisional Detective,	1	9	0	1	13	0
2nd Class Ordinary Sergeants,	1	9	0	1	14	0
1st " "	1	13	0	1	16	0
2nd " Reserve "	1	13	0	1	17	0
1st " "	1	16	0	1	19	0
Station Divisional Detectives and Clerk Sergeants,	1	18	0	1	19	0
2nd Class Detective Sergeants at Chief Office,	2	2	0	2	2	0
1st " " " "	2	2	0	2	7	0
2nd " Ordinary Inspectors,	2	17	0	3	2	0
2nd " Reserve "	3	4	0	3	11	0
1st " Ordinary "	3	9	0	3	13	0
1st " Reserve "	3	19	0	3	3	0
Chief Inspector,	3	16	0	3	6	0
Detective Inspectors at Chief Office,	3	5	0	3	9	0
Chief Detective Inspectors,	3	16	11	4	8	11
	4	14	2	4	19	0

Superintendents up to 11th inst., received £250 per annum, increasing by £10 annually to £330; they now receive £400, increasing by £10 annually to £400. Deductions are made for income tax, and 2½ per cent for superannuation.

THOMAS KITTLE, Superintendent.

Metropolitan Police Office,
4, Whitehall-place,
23rd November, 1872.

ENCLOSURE B.

METROPOLITAN POLICE FORCE.

CONDITIONS UPON WHICH EACH CONSTABLE IS ADMITTED.

1st. Each constable is to devote his whole time to the police service. He is not to carry on any trade, nor can his wife be allowed to keep a shop.

2nd. He is to serve and reside wherever he is appointed.

3rd. He is to appear in his police dress at all times when on duty, but he may wear plain clothes when off duty, unless directed to the contrary.

4th. He is promptly to obey all lawful orders from the persons in authority over him.

5th. He is to obey all the regulations of the service.

6th. Such debts owing by him, as the Commissioner directs to be paid, shall be paid by him forthwith.

7th. A deduction of one shilling will be made from his pay, each day, when certified by the surgeon sick and unfit for duty, except in certain cases, when full pay is allowed by the Commissioner.

8th. A deduction of one shilling a week is to be made from his pay, if unmarried.*

9th. If married, according to a regulated scale for the accommodation provided.*

10th. If single, and so directed, he shall on entering, furnish himself with a box of the pattern approved by the Commissioner, of the following dimensions, viz. :—Exterior measurement, length, 30 inches; breadth, 18½ inches; depth, 14½ inches; flat top.*

11th. He shall not resign nor withdraw himself from his duties, unless allowed to do so in writing by the Superintendent of the division or by the Commissioner; nor unless he shall have given to his Superintendent one month's previous notice in writing. If he resign or withdraw without such leave or notice, he is liable to forfeit all pay then due or pay a penalty of Five Pounds.

12th. Each police constable is liable to immediate dismissal for unfitness, negligence, or misconduct, independently of any other punishment to which by law he may be subject. The Commissioner may also remove him from the service by dismissal or otherwise without assigning any reason. If he be dismissed the police force, the whole of his pay then due is forfeited.

13th. A constable dismissed from the police force, or who resigns his situation, shall, immediately after the dismissal or resignation, deliver up every article of dress and appointments which have been supplied to him. If any such articles or appointments have, in the opinion of the Commissioner, been improperly used or damaged, a deduction from the pay then due to the party shall be made, sufficient to make good the damage or supply a new article.

14th. A certificate of good conduct in the police force will be given by the Commissioner, subject to the regulations of the service.

15th. Every police constable in the force may hope to rise, by activity, intelligence, and good conduct, to the superior stations.

16th. He receives his pay each Wednesday, for the week ending the Sunday before.

17th. His pay, on being appointed constable, is 24s. per week; when advanced to the second class 27s. per week, and to the first class 30s. per week. In addition to his pay, the following articles of uniform clothing will be supplied to him, viz.:—

FIRST YEAR.

1 great coat.   2 pairs of boots.
1 dress tunic.   1 police helmet.
1 cape.   1 stock.
2 pairs of trousers.   1 armlet.

SECOND YEAR.

1 dress tunic.
2 pairs of trousers.
2 pairs of boots.
1 police helmet.

Coals.—Single men living in section houses are allowed weekly 20lbs. in summer and 40lbs. in winter, but a money allowance in lieu of coals is given to married men, and to single men living out of section houses.

18th. A gratuity or pension may be granted by the Secretary of State according to the following scale :—

1st. Gratuity of one month's pay for each year's service after five years and less than fifteen years.

2nd. Pensions on fifteen years' service completed, fifteen-fiftieths of the pay may be granted, and an increase of one-fiftieth for each successive year up to thirty years' service completed.

3rd. Pensions to men under the age of sixty years, and for less than thirty years' service, are to be granted for a term of five years only, the Commissioner being empowered to recommend the grant for a longer period of years, or for life, in a case of extraordinary merit or good conduct, taking the length of service also into account.

4th. After thirty years' service, or the age of sixty years of the party, the pension to be for life, and equal to thirty-fiftieths of the pay, or a larger proportion in cases of extraordinary merit or good conduct.

5th. For injuries received at any time in the actual performance of duty, a pension for life may be granted of an amount in proportion to the resulting disability, but not exceeding the full pay; the grounds of disability are to be carefully investigated and fully set forth.

6th. A pension, retiring allowance, or gratuity is not to be granted in any case except on the certificate of the chief surgeon, that the party is from mental or bodily incapacity unable to perform his duty any longer, and the certificate of the Commissioner that he has served with zeal and fidelity.

19th. A pension or retiring allowance is granted only upon the condition that it becomes forfeited, and may be

* When lodgings are provided.

withdrawn by the Secretary of State, in any of the following cases :—

   1st. On conviction of the grantee for any indictable offence ;

   2nd. On his knowingly associating with thieves or suspected persons ;

   3rd. On his refusing to give information and assistance to the police whenever in his power, for the detection and apprehension of criminals, and for the suppression of any disturbance of the public peace ;

   4th. If he enter into or continue to carry on any business, occupation, or employment which shall be, in the opinion of the Secretary of State, disgraceful itself, or injurious to the public, or in which he shall make use of the fact of his former employment in the police in a manner which the Secretary of State considers to be discreditable and improper.

The law (2nd and 3rd Vict. c. 47, s. 23) does not entitle any constable absolutely to any superannuation allowance, nor prevent him from being dismissed without superannuation allowance.

APPENDIX IX.

Average Prices in Dublin of Bread, Oatmeal, Potatoes, and Beef, compiled from the Quarterly Returns of the Registrar-General

Year.	Quarter.	Bread, 4 lb. Loaf.	Oatmeal, per cwt.	Potatoes, per cwt.	Beef (Dublin Cattle Market, per cwt.)	Year.	Quarter.	Bread, 4 lb. Loaf.	Oatmeal, per cwt.	Potatoes, per cwt.	Beef (Dublin Cattle Market, per cwt.)

(table values illegible)

Summary of the Years 1864 to 1871.

Year.	Bread, 4 lb. Loaf.	Oatmeal, per cwt.	Potatoes, per cwt.	Beef (Dublin Cattle Market), per cwt.
1864,				
1865,				
1866,				
1867,				
1868,				
1869,				
1870,				
1871,				

(table values illegible)

www.ingramcontent.com/pod-product-compliance
Lightning Source LLC
Chambersburg PA
CBHW022027080426
42733CB00007B/752